R 423

Black's Writing Dictionary

T. J. Hulme   T. F. Carmody   J. A. Hulme

A and C Black   ·   London

The compilation of this dictionary has been helped
considerably by the many class teachers who have
co-operated with us. We are most grateful for their
help, and for the help given by various Primary and
Secondary School Head Teachers, College of Education
Lecturers and, most of all, by the children themselves

TJH   TFC   JAH

Published by A and C Black (Publishers) Limited
35 Bedford Row, London WC1R 4JH
as a new and expanded edition of the *Junior Writing Dictionary*
first published in 1962.

© 1962 and 1972 T J Hulme, T F Carmody and
J A Hulme

Reprinted 1973, 1974, 1976, 1977, 1978,
1980, 1982, 1986, 1988, 1990, 1993, 1996

A CIP catalogue record for this book
is available from the British Library.

ISBN 0-7136-1272-X limp

Printed and bound in Great Britain by
BPC Books Ltd
A member of
The British Printing Company Ltd

Contents

Preface   7

How to use this book   9

The dictionary   11

The following list shows the page number
for each new letter of the alphabet:

a	11	j	99	s	159
b	19	k	101	t	193
c	33	l	104	u	207
d	53	m	113	v	210
e	63	n	123	w	212
f	69	o	126	x	220
g	80	p	130	y	220
h	87	q	147	z	221
i	96	r	148		

Useful information   222

Preface

A dictionary has, in our experience, two main uses: as a reference book for meaning and as a reference book for correct spelling.

Black's Writing Dictionary is designed to help children in their written work, so that they may spell words accurately and may understand their use and meaning. It is also intended to serve as a preparation for the more advanced dictionary at a later stage.

To achieve these aims, three principles have been borne in mind:

1. Those words which the child needs should be included, together with a lesser number of more difficult words which will help to increase vocabulary.

2. All words must be easy to find and their meanings must be easy to understand.

3. The pattern must be consistent so that the child will be able to use the dictionary with confidence and safety.

Many years of observation of word frequency in school written work, and extensive research, form the background to the choice of words. With the increasing impact of television and space research news it has been necessary to include many words which have only recently become part of the everyday vocabulary.

The range of words has been limited in order not to complicate the dictionary. In any case, the child who needs less common words is generally capable of using a more advanced dictionary.

The simple layout and the clear word lists are designed to make the words easy to find. Where a word has more than one meaning, only the most common meanings are given.

The three columns of each page contain:

1 the basic words (printed in red);

2 their simple definitions (with noun senses of a word preceding verb senses);

3 their derivatives, in alphabetical order.

The derivatives included are those words which come from the parent word and which the child frequently uses, e.g. the word **act** has **acted** and **acting**; the word **announce** has **announced**, **announcement**, **announcer** and **announcing**.

Where the meaning of a derivative cannot easily be deduced from the meaning of the parent word, the derivative has been listed as a parent word and defined, e.g., the word **assistant** is derived from the word **assist**, but it has been defined separately because of its special meaning.

As plurals are so commonly misspelt, the plurals that do not simply add 's' to the singular are listed in the right-hand column and printed in red.

All third person singulars that do not simply add 's' are listed together with the past and present participles. But where the verb also has a noun meaning, both the plural and third person singular are included, e.g., **address** has **addresses** as its plural but it also has **addressed**, **addresses** and **addressing** as its other derivatives.

Where a derivative differs greatly in form from the parent word it is listed in normal alphabetical order in column 1 and used in a sentence to illustrate its meaning; e.g., the verb **bring** has **brought** as one of its derivatives; **brought** is also listed in column 1 and used in a sentence.

We feel sure that the 8000 words listed in this book cover most of the words that the child will need, whether they be past or present participles, irregular verb spellings, infinitives, adjectives, adverbs, comparatives or superlatives, or irregularly spelt plurals. This comprehensive list ensures that the child will be able to correct his spelling mistakes unaided or with the minimum of help from the teacher.

By making it easy for the child to find the words he needs, he will be encouraged to use the dictionary more frequently and so will acquire the skill and confidence necessary to encourage him to proceed to the more advanced type of dictionary.

TJH
TFC
JAH

How to use this book

This book gives you most of the spellings and meanings you need in your reading and writing. By using it often you will quickly be able to find the word you need.

Here is the way to begin.

Suppose you waht to find the word **aboard** Its first letter is 'a' so turn to the part of the book marked **a** Then go down the list of words in red on the left-hand side of the page until you come to

aboard   on a ship

If you want to find the word **appetite** turn to the part marked **a**. You could go through every word until you came to the word **appetite** But this would take a long time and there is a quicker way.

The first two letters of **appetite** are **ap**. Find the part marked **a**, and look at the top of the page at the small letters. When you find the page that has the small letters **ap** look down that page until you come to

appetite   a wish to have food

Sometimes the exact word you want will not be on the left-hand side of the page. In that case, look on the right-hand side of the page and you will probably find it there, printed in black.

You will notice something else if you look at the words on the right. Some of them are printed in red.

As you know, the words for most things need only an 's' to make them plural; **dog** becomes **dogs**, **cow** becomes **cows**, and so on. But some words do not add 's' and the plurals of these words are printed in red, like this:

cargo   a ship's load   **cargoes**

Use your dictionary every time you want to know how to spell a word, or when you want to know its meaning. When you have found it, learn what it means and how to spell it. It will save your looking it up next time.

a

abacus	a frame with beads on wires, to help with counting	**abaci** **abacuses**
abandon	1. to leave somebody or something, meaning never to return 2. to stop doing something before you have finished	**abandoned** **abandoning**
abbey	a place where monks or nuns live, or where they used to live	**abbess** **abbot**
able	1. clever 2. can do something	**ability**
aboard	on a ship	
about	1. almost or nearly 2. to do with 3. around	
above	over	
abroad	in another country across the sea	
absence	being away	**absentee**
absent	away	
accept	to take what is given to you	**acceptance** **accepted** **accepting**
accident	something unpleasant that happens by mistake	**accidental** **accidentally**
account	1. a story 2. a bill	
accurate	exactly right	**accurately**
ache	1. a lasting pain 2. to have a pain that lasts	**ached** **aching**
acid	1. a very sour liquid 2. sour	
acorn	fruit of the oak tree	
acre	a piece of land the size of a small football pitch: 4840 square yards	

acrobat	a person who does clever tricks with his body, often in a circus	
across	1. from side to side 2. on the other side	
act	1. something that you do 2. to do something 3. to take part in a play	**acted** **acting** **action** **active** **activity**
actor	a man who takes part in plays or films	
actress	a woman who takes part in plays or films	**actresses**
add	1. to find the sum of two or more numbers 2. to join one thing to another	**added** **adding** **addition**
adder	a small poisonous snake: a viper	
address	1. the place where someone lives 2. to write an address 3. to speak to	**addresses** **addressed** **addresses** **addressing**
adhesive	paste for sticking things together	
admiral	a very important officer in the navy	
admire	to think a lot of	**admirable** **admiration** **admired** **admiring**
admit	1. to let someone or something in 2. to own up	**admission** **admitted** **admitting**
adult	a grown-up person	
advance	to go forward	**advanced** **advancing**
advantage	something that helps or is useful	
adventure	an exciting time	**adventurous**

advertise	to make something well-known, usually through posters and newspapers	**advertised** **advertisement** **advertising**
advise	to tell a person something in order to help him	**advice** **advised** **advising**
aerial	wire rods, often on a roof, for a radio or television set	
aerodrome	level ground where aeroplanes take off and land	
aeroplane	a machine which flies in the air	
affectionate	loving	**affectionately**
afford	to be able to spend time or money	**afforded** **affording**
afraid	frightened	
after	behind: later	
afternoon	between noon and evening	
afterwards	later on	
again	once more	
against	1. on the opposite side to 2. touching; near to	
agree	to think the same as	**agreeable** **agreed** **agreeing**
aground	stuck on the sand or rock in a ship	
ahead	in front	
aid	1. help given to someone 2. to help someone	**aided** **aiding**
aim	to get ready to hit	**aimed** **aiming**
air	1. what we breathe 2. to make sure that clothes are quite dry	**aired** **airing**
aircraft	flying machine	**aircraft**
airfield	place where aircraft take off and land	

air-hostess	someone who looks after passengers on an aircraft	air-hostesses
airpilot	one of the crew of an aeroplane	
airport	a place where passenger aircraft take off and land	
ajar	open a little	
alarm	1. fear 2. a noise or shout to warn people of danger 3. to frighten	alarmed alarming
album	a book for storing stamps or pictures	
alight	1. on fire 2. to step down from something	alighted alighting
alike	the same, or nearly the same, as	
alley	a narrow path between buildings	alleyway
alligator	a short-nosed crocodile	
allotment	a piece of land used as an extra garden, usually for growing vegetables	
allow	to let: to give permission	allowed allowing
alloy	a mixture of metals	
almost	nearly	
alone	by oneself	
along	from one end to the other	
aloud	so that someone can hear	
alphabet	all the letters from A to Z	alphabetical
already	by now	
also	as well	
altar	the holy table in a church	
alter	to change	alteration altered altering
although	even if: though	

altogether	completely	
aluminium	a very light metal	
always	1. at all times 2. every time	
amaze	to surprise very much	**amazed** **amazement** **amazing**
ambulance	a van for carrying sick people	
among	with other things or people	
amount	a quantity	
amuse	to make people laugh	**amused** **amusement**
amuse oneself	to pass the time pleasantly	**amusing**
anchor	1. a large hook which digs into the sea bed to hold a ship 2. to drop anchor	**anchored** **anchoring**
ancient	very old	
angel	a spirit sent from God	
anger	bad temper: rage	**angrily** **angry**
angle	a corner	
animal	a live creature	
ankle	the joint between foot and leg	
announce	to tell something to a group of people	**announced** **announce-** **ment** **announcer** **announcing**
annoy	to make someone cross	**annoyance** **annoyed** **annoying**
annual	1. a book which comes out once a year 2. once a year	**annually**
anorak	a waterproof jacket with hood	
another	1. a different one 2. one more	

answer	1. a reply: the result of a sum 2. to reply	**answered** **answering**
antelope	an animal like a deer	
anxious	worried	**anxiously**
any	one, or some, of a number of things	**anybody** **anyhow** **anyone** **anything** **anyway**
apart	not together	
ape	a monkey	
apologise	to say you are sorry	**apologised** **apologising**
apology	what you say to show you are sorry	**apologies**
appear	1. to come into sight 2. to seem	**appearance** **appeared** **appearing**
appetite	a wish to have food	
apple	a fruit	
approach	to get near to	**approached** **approaches** **approaching**
approximate	almost correct	**approxi-** **mately** **approxima-** **tion**
apricot	a fruit	
April	the fourth month of the year	
apron	a cloth tied round the waist to keep one's clothes clean	
aquarium	a fish-tank	
arc	part of a curve or circle	
arch	the curved top of a bridge, door or window	**arches** **archway**
archer	a person who shoots with a bow and arrow	**archery**
area	the size of a flat space	
argue	to talk for and against something	**argued** **arguing** **argument**

arithmetic	working with numbers	
arm	1. the part of the body between the hand and the shoulder	**armed**
	2. to give weapons to	**arming**
armour	a suit to protect the body in battle	**armoured**
army	a lot of soldiers	**armies**
around	on every side	
arrange	to put in order: to plan	**arranged** **arrangement** **arranging**
arrest	to take as prisoner	**arrested** **arresting**
arrive	to reach a place	**arrival** **arrived** **arriving**
arrow	used with a bow for shooting	
artful	crafty	
artificial	not real: made up	
artist	a person who paints, or draws or carves	**artistic**
ash	1. what is left when something has been burnt	**ashes**
	2. a kind of tree	
ashamed	sorry for something you have done	
ashore	on land	
ask	to put a question	**asked** **asking**
asleep	not awake: sleeping	
aspirin	a medicine that helps to stop pain	
ass	a donkey	**asses**
assembly	a gathering of people	**assemblies**
assist	to help	**assistance** **assisted** **assisting**

assistant	1. someone who serves in a shop 2. someone who helps	
astonish	to surprise	**astonished** **astonishes** **astonishing** **astonish-** **ment**
astronaut	someone who travels in space	
astronomy	the study of stars and planets	**astronomer**
astride	with legs apart	
ate	(Peter *ate* his dinner quickly)	
atlas	a book of maps	**atlases**
atmosphere	the air surrounding a planet	
atom	a very, very tiny piece	**atomic**
attack	to start a fight	**attacked** **attacking**
attempt	1. a try 2. to try to do something	**attempted** **attempting**
attend	to be there	**attendance** **attended** **attending**
attendant	a person who is paid to look after a place that people use, such as a park or a swimming bath	
attention	1. taking notice 2. standing straight up with feet together and arms by your sides	
attic	a room in a roof	
attract	1. to be very pleasing to people 2. to make things come closer	**attracted** **attracting** **attraction** **attractive**
audience	people who are listening or watching a performance	
August	the eighth month of the year	
aunt	your mother's or father's sister or your uncle's wife	**auntie** **aunty**

author	a person who writes books or plays
autograph	someone's name in his or her own handwriting
autumn	between summer and winter
avalanche	a lot of snow and ice sliding down a mountain
avenue	a road, usually lined with trees
average	the middle point between the the highest and the lowest
avoid	1. to keep away from **avoided** 2. to move so that something **avoiding** misses you
awake	not sleeping
away	not here
awful	terrible **awfully**
awkward	1. clumsy 2. difficult to handle
axe	a chopper
axis	the line or point round which **axes** something turns
axle	a rod on which a wheel turns

b

baboon	a large monkey
baby	a very young child **babies**
back	1. the opposite side to the **backed** front **background** 2. a defender in a game **backing** 3. to move backwards **backwards** 4. to give support to
bacon	part of the meat we get from pigs

ba

bacteria	very small living things which cause disease
badge	a decoration we wear on clothes to show that we belong to a special group, such as a club or school
badger	a hairy animal about as big as a small dog, which digs holes in the ground in which to live
bails	the two bits of wood placed on top of cricket stumps
bake	to cook food in an oven **baked baking**
baker	a person who makes bread and cakes
bakery	a place where bread and cakes **bakeries** are made
balance	1. to keep something steady in **balanced** one position **balancing** 2. scales for weighing or comparing masses
balcony	1. a platform that sticks out **balconies** high up on a wall 2. the top floor in a cinema or theatre
bald	with no hair
ball	1. a round object used in playing games 2. a dancing party **ballroom**
ballet	a special kind of dancing **ballerina**
balloon	a very thin rubber bag which can be blown up
banana	a fruit with a yellow skin
band	1. a thin strip of something 2. a number of people making **bandstand** music together 3. a group of people
bandage	1. a strip of cloth for covering **bandaged** a cut **bandaging** 2. to tie up a cut or sore

bandit	a robber
bang	1. a loud, sudden noise 2. to make a loud, sudden **banged** noise **banging** 3. to hit
bangle	a metal ring worn on the wrist
banisters	the handrail at the side of the stairs
banjo	a musical instrument

bank	1. a building where money is **banker**
	    kept safe
	2. the ground at the side of a
	    river
	3. sloping ground

banner	a flag
barber	a person who cuts men's hair

bare	not covered **bareback**
	                            barefoot
	                            bareheaded
	                            barely

bargain	something bought cheaply
barge	a large, flat cargo boat used mainly on rivers and canals
bark	1. the outer covering of a tree 2. a noise made by a dog **barked** 3. to make a noise like a dog **barking**
barley	a kind of corn used to make beer
barn	a farm building for storing crops

barrel	1. a round, wooden container
	    for liquids
	2. the long, narrow tube of a
	    gun

barrow	a small hand-cart
base	1. the bottom of something 2. place where a ship or air- craft is kept
basement	part of a building below ground-level

basket	a bag, made from cane, for carrying things
basketball	a game similar to netball
bassoon	a musical wind instrument
bat	1. a mouse-like animal that flies at night
	2. a piece of wood used to hit a ball **batted**
	3. to have an innings at cricket **batting**
bath	1. a tub for water in which you **bathed** can wash your body **bathing**
	2. to wash a child or animal **bathroom**
bathe	to go into the sea or river to **bathed** swim **bathing**
batsman	a person who is batting in a **batsmen** game
battery	a container for storing elec-**batteries** tricity
battle	a fight between two opposite **battlefield** sides **battleship**
bay	part of the sea which makes a curve into the land
bazaar	1. an eastern market
	2. a sale to get money for helping people
beach	the sand or stones at the edge **beaches** of the sea
bead	a small shape which can be threaded on a string
beak	the hard part of a bird's mouth
beam	1. a thick, heavy bar of wood
	2. a ray of light **beamed**
	3. to shine **beaming**
bean	a kidney-shaped seed in a pod, used as a vegetable
bear	1. a strong, hairy wild animal
	2. to carry **bearing**
	3. to suffer **bore**
beard	the hair on the chin and cheeks **bearded**
beast	any large four-footed animal **beastly**

beat	1. the district looked after by one police constable	
	2. to hit	**beaten**
	3. to stir quickly	**beating**
	4. to do better than someone else	
beauty	1. a lovely thing	
	2. loveliness	**beautiful**
		beautifully
beaver	an animal that lives in or near water	
because	for this reason	
become	to grow to be: to come to be	**became**
		becoming
bed	1. a thing to sleep on	**bedclothes**
	2. a garden plot	**bedroom**
		bedside
		bedspread
		bedstead
		bedtime
bee	the insect from which we get honey	
beech	a tree with a smooth grey bark	
beef	meat from bulls or cows	
been	(I have *been* busy today)	
beer	a drink made from malt, barley and hops	
beetle	an insect with hard wing covers	
before	in front of: earlier	
beg	to ask for money, clothes or food	**begged**
		begging
began	(It *began* to rain so I went home)	
beggar	a person who begs because of being poor	
begin	to start	**began**
		beginner
		beginning
		begun

behave	1. to do as you are told 2. to be good in front of others	**behaved** **behaving** **behaviour**
behead	to cut off the head	**beheaded** **beheading**
behind	at the back of: late	
being	(You are *being* good if you are behaving yourself)	
believe	to think that something is true	**belief** **believed** **believing**
bell	a metal cup, which rings when it is hit	
belong	to be part of	**belonged** **belonging**
belong to	to be owned by someone or to be part of something	
below	under: lower than	
belt	a strap which goes round the waist	
bench	1. a long seat 2. a strong table	**benches**
bend	1. a curve 2. to curve	**bending** **bent**
beneath	under	
beret	a soft cap with no peak	
berry	a small fruit which has seeds	**berries**
beside	at the side of	
besides	as well as	
best	the finest	
betray	1. to give away a secret to an enemy 2. to do or say something that you have promised not to	**betrayal** **betrayed** **betraying**
better	improved: not so ill	
between	in the middle	
beware	be careful	
beyond	further than	

bible	a collection of books about the life of Jesus Christ and the times before He was born	
bicycle	a riding machine with two wheels	
big	large	**bigger** **biggest**
bill	1. a bird's beak 2. a note showing how much money is owing	
binary	a scale of numbers using two as a base instead of ten	
bind	to fasten together	**binding** **bound**
birch	a tree with a smooth silvery bark	**birches**
bird	a feathered animal that flies	
birth	1. the start of one's life 2. the beginning	**birthday**
biscuit	a small thin, crisp cake	
bisect	to cut into two equal parts	**bisected** **bisecting** **bisection**
bishop	an important member of the clergy	
bit	1. a small piece 2. the metal part of a bridle, which fits into a horse's mouth	
bite	to cut with your teeth	**bit** **biting** **bitten**
bitter	sour or sharp	
black	the opposite of white: very dark	
blackberry	a small black fruit, often found in hedgerows	**blackberries** **blackberry-ing**
blackbird	a black-feathered bird	
blackboard	a board on which you write with chalk	

blackcurrant	a small black fruit, grown on a garden bush
blacksmith	a person who makes things with iron, such as shoes for horses
blade	1. the cutting part of a knife 2. a piece of grass
blame	to say that it is someone else's fault **blamed** **blaming**
blancmange	a kind of jelly made with cornflour and milk
blank	without any writing on: empty
blanket	a woollen covering on a bed
blast	a rush of air: an explosion
blast-off	the take-off of a space rocket
blaze	1. a fire with bright flames **blazed** 2. to burn strongly **blazing**
blazer	a flannel sports jacket, often part of a school uniform
bleed	to lose blood from a cut **bled** **bleeding**
blew	(The referee *blew* the whistle)
blind	1. a screen for a window 2. unable to see **blinded** **blinding**
blindfold	with the eyes covered **blindfolded**
blink	to open and close one's eyes quickly **blinked** **blinking**
blister	a swelling, like a bubble, on the skin
blizzard	a driving snowstorm
block	1. a large, solid piece of some-thing **blocked** 2. to close up **blocking**
blond	fair haired
blood	the red liquid in our bodies
blossom	1. a flower **blossomed** 2. to flower **blossoming**

blot	1. a spot, or smudge, of ink 2. to dry up ink	**blotted** **blotter** **blotting**
blouse	a loose top part of a woman's clothing	
blow	1. a hard knock 2. to send out air from your mouth	**blew** **blowing** **blown**
blue	the colour of a cloudless sky	
bluebell	a wild flower	
bluebottle	a large fly	
blunt	not sharp	
blush	to go red in the face, usually because you are shy	blushes **blushed** **blushes** **blushing**
board	1. a plank of wood 2. to get on to something that moves	**boarded** **boarding**
boarder	1. a child who lives at school except during the holidays 2. someone who lodges in another person's house	
boast	to make out that you are better than you are	**boasted** **boasting**
boat	a small ship	**boating**
body	1. a living person 2. the main part of anything	**bodies** **bodyguard**
bog	wet, spongy ground	**boggy**
boil	1. a painful swelling under the skin 2. to heat any liquid until it bubbles	**boiled** **boiler** **boiling**
bold	fearless	**boldly**
bolt	1. a sliding fastener, often on a door 2. to run off suddenly 3. to gobble one's food	**bolted** **bolting**

bomb	1. something filled with explosive 2. to drop a bomb	**bombed** **bombing**
bomber	an aeroplane that carries bombs	
bone	part of the skeleton of the body	**bony**
bonfire	a fire lit outside, usually in a garden	
bonnet	1. a woman's hat that ties on with ribbons 2. the part of the car that covers the engine	
book	1. sheets of paper fastened together in a cover 2. to order in advance	**booked** **booking**
bookcase	a set of shelves for holding books	
boot	1. a cover for the ankle and foot 2. the back part of a car, in which luggage is carried	
border	the edge	
bore	1. to make a hole in 2. to talk in an uninteresting way	**bored** **boring**
born	(Jane was *born* in London ten years ago)	
borrow	to get something on loan	**borrowed** **borrowing**
both	the two together	
bother	1. trouble 2. to worry or trouble	**bothered** **bothering**
bottle	a glass container for liquids	
bottom	the lowest part	
bough	a branch of a tree	
bought	(I *bought* some sweets at the shop)	
bounce	to spring up and down	**bounced** **bouncing**

bound	1. a leap 2. tied up
bound for	on the way to
boundary	a mark to show the outside **boundaries** edge
bow	1. the front of a ship 2. a weapon for shooting arrows 3. used with a violin to make **bowed** music **bowing** 4. a knot with two loops 5. to bend forward
bowl	1. a deep dish 2. to send a ball along **bowled** **bowler** **bowling**
box	1. a container **boxes** 2. to fight with fists **boxed** **boxer** **boxes** **boxing**
boy	a male child
bracelet	a ring worn on the wrist
braces	straps to hold up trousers
braid	a woven band
brain	the part inside the head with **brainy** which you think
brake	1. the part of a machine that **braked** slows it down **braking** 2. to slow anything down
branch	part of a tree **branches**
brass	a yellow-coloured metal
brave	full of courage **bravely** **braver** **bravery** **bravest**
bread	food made mostly of flour and baked in an oven
break	1. a crack or hole **breakable** 2. a rest **breaking** 3. to shatter: to crack **broke** **broken**

breakdown	when something will not work
breakfast	the first meal of the day
breakwater	a wall that is built to break the force of the waves
breast	the front part of the body, between the neck and stomach
breath	air that goes in and out of the lungs **breathless**
breathe	to take air in and out of the lungs **breathed breathing**
breeze	a gentle wind **breezy**
brick	a block of baked clay
bricklayer	a person who builds with bricks
bride	a woman on her wedding-day
bridegroom	a man on his wedding-day
bridesmaid	a bride's attendant
bridge	1. a path or road built over a road or river or railway line 2. the place on a ship where the captain stands
bridle	part of the harness that goes over a horse's head
bright	shining **brighter brightest brightly**
brilliant	very bright **brilliantly**
brim	1. the top edge of something, such as a cup or glass 2. the part that sticks out around the main part of a hat
bring	to fetch or carry **bringing brought**
bristle	stiff hair used in brushes **bristly**
brittle	easily broken
broad	wide **broader broadest**
broadcast	1. to send out over the radio 2. to scatter freely **broadcasting**

broke	(I *broke* my pencil by biting it)	
broken	(She has *broken* her train by dropping it on the floor)	
brooch	an ornament to pin on a dress	brooches
brook	a small stream	
broom	a long-handled brush	**broomstick**
brother	(I have one *brother*, David, and one sister, Joanna)	
brought	(John *brought* his satchel to school yesterday)	
brown	the colour of chocolate	
bruise	1. a dark mark made by knocking the skin 2. to make a bruise on something	**bruised** **bruising**
brush	1. hairs or bristles fixed to a handle, for brushing or sweeping 2. to rub with a brush	brushes **brushed** brushes **brushing**
bubble	1. air with a skin of liquid 2. to cause bubbles	**bubbled** **bubbling**
bucket	a pail, usually for carrying water	**bucketful**
buckle	1. a fastening on a belt or shoe 2. to crumple something	**buckled** **buckling**
budgerigar	a brightly-coloured cage-bird	
buffalo	a kind of wild ox	**buffaloes**
buffer	strong spring which softens the blow when railway carriages or trucks hit each other	
bugle	a musical instrument like a small trumpet	**bugler**
build	to make something: to put something together	**building** **built**
builder	a person who builds	
building	something that is built	
bulb	1. a round-shaped root 2. an electric light	
bulge	1. a swelling 2. to swell out	**bulged** **bulging**

bu

bull a male cow

bulldozer a powerful machine for level-ling ground

bullet a small piece of metal fired from a gun

bully
1. someone who hurts or frightens people **bullies** **bullied**
2. to act like a bully **bullies** **bullying**

bump
1. a knock or blow **bumped**
2. to knock into **bumping** **bumpy**

bumper a metal bar across the front or back of a car to protect it

bunch a group of things together, such as flowers **bunches**

bundle several things fastened to-gether

bungalow a house with no upstairs

bunk
1. a narrow bed fixed to the wall in a ship's cabin
2. beds, one above the other

buoy a marker floating in the sea to guide ships

burglar someone who breaks into a building at night to steal **burglary**

burn
1. the mark caused by some-thing very hot **burned** **burning**
2. to be on fire **burnt**

burrow
1. a hole in the ground made by an animal **burrowed** **burrowing**
2. to tunnel in the ground, like a rabbit

burst to break apart suddenly **bursting**

bury to place, or hide, beneath the ground **burial** **buried** **buries** **burying**

bus a motor-coach **buses**

bush	a small, thick-growing tree	**bushes** **bushy**
business	trade or work	**businesses**
busy	active, doing something	**busier** **busiest** **busily**
busybody	someone who will not mind his own business	**busybodies**
butcher	a person who sells meat	
butter	a food made from milk	**buttered** **buttering**
buttercup	a small yellow wild flower	
butterfly	an insect with large, brightly-coloured wings	**butterflies**
button	1. a fastening for clothes 2. to fasten with a button	**buttoned** **buttonhole** **buttoning**
buy	to get something by paying money	**bought** **buying**
buzz	1. a noise made by a bee 2. to make a noise like a bee	**buzzed** **buzzer** **buzzes** **buzzing**
by-pass	a road made for traffic to avoid a busy place	**by-passes**

cabbage	a vegetable with green leaves
cabin	1. a wooden hut 2. a small room in a ship
cabinet	a kind of cupboard
cable	1. a very strong rope, often made of wire 2. a wire for carrying electricity
cactus	a prickly plant

cacti

café	a place where light meals are served	
cage	a place in which birds or animals are kept	
cake	a sweet loaf, often with currants	
calculate	to count or find out using mathematics	**calculated** **calculating** **calculation**
calendar	a list of the days, weeks and months of the year	
calf	1. a young bull or cow 2. the back of the leg	**calves**
call	1. to shout 2. to visit someone	**called** **caller** **calling**
calm	1. peaceful: smooth 2. to make peaceful	**calmed** **calmer** **calmest** **calming** **calmly**
came	(My uncle *came* to see me yesterday)	
camel	a large animal which has either one or two humps	
camera	a box into which you put film in order to take photographs	
camp	1. a number of tents or huts for people to live in 2. to live in a camp	**camped** **camper** **camping**
canal	an artificially made waterway for boats and ships	
canary	a small yellow-feathered bird that sings	**canaries**
candle	a stick of wax which burns to give light	**candlestick**
cane	1. the thick hollow stem of reeds or grasses 2. to hit anyone with a cane	**caned** **caning**

cannibal   a person who eats the flesh of other people

cannon
1. a large mounted gun used in olden times
2. a light quick-firing gun

cannot   (If I close my eyes I *cannot* see)

canoe   a narrow boat that is paddled along

canteen   a room in a school, office or factory where meals are cooked and served

canvas   strong, coarse cloth

canyon   a very deep valley with steep rocky sides

capacity   the amount of space inside something

capital
1. the chief city in a country
2. a large letter of the alphabet

capsize   to overturn a boat   capsized capsizing

capsule   the part of a space ship in which the astronauts travel

captain
1. a leader of a team
2. an officer in the army or navy

capture   to take as prisoner   captive captured capturing

caravan   a small house on wheels

card   stiff paper

cardboard   stiff board made of paper

cardigan   a woollen jacket

care
1. caution: being careful
2. worry
3. to bother about
   cared careful carefully

care for   to look after   careless carelessly carelessness caring

caretaker	someone who looks after a school or office	
cargo	a ship's load	**cargoes**
carnival	a happy and noisy party in fancy dress	
carol	a special hymn for Christmas	
carpenter	a person who works with wood	**carpentry**
carpet	a soft covering for the floor	
carriage	a coach for the road or the railway	
carrot	an orange-coloured root vegetable	
carry	to take from one place to another	**carried** **carries** **carrying**
carry on	to continue	
cart	a wagon	
carton	a container in which things are packed	
cartoon	a funny drawing, on paper or in the form of a short film	
carve	1. to cut meat 2. to shape wood or stone by cutting	**carved** **carving**
case	a box	
cash	money	
cashier	a person who is in charge of money	
castaway	a person who has been ship-wrecked in a lonely place	
castle	a fortress	
catapult	a forked stick with elastic used for shooting stones	
catch	1. a lock 2. to grasp something which has been thrown	**catches** **catching** **caught**

catch up	to reach	
caterpillar	the grub from which a moth or butterfly comes	
cathedral	a very large church	
catkin	the flower of the hazel, willow and some other trees	
cattle	farm animals	
caught	(He threw the ball and I *caught* it)	
cauliflower	a kind of flowering cabbage	
cause	to make something happen	**caused** **causing**
caution	care	**cautious** **cautiously**
cave	a large hollow in the side of a hill or cliff, or underground	
cedar	an evergreen tree	
ceiling	the roof of a room	
celery	a vegetable which we eat	
cell	1. a very tiny part of all living things 2. a room in a prison or monastery 3. a part of a battery	
cellar	a room under the ground	
cellophane	a transparent material for wrapping things	
cement	a powder used for making concrete	
cemetery	a graveyard	**cemeteries**
centimetre	a measure of length in the metric system. One hundredth of a metre.	
centipede	a crawling insect with many feet	
centre	the middle	**central**
century	1. one hundred years 2. one hundred runs at cricket	**centuries**

cereal	1. a grain used as food 2. a breakfast food	
certain	sure	
certificate	a piece of writing which proves that something is true	
chain	1. links, usually of metal, joined together 2. to fasten with a chain	**chained** **chaining**
chair	a seat with a back	
chalk	a soft stone which can be used for writing	**chalked** **chalking** **chalky**
chameleon	a kind of lizard which can change colour	
champion	the winner of the final in a sport or game	**champion-ship**
chance	luck: something not planned	
change	1. money which you get back when you have paid too much 2. to alter 3. to put one thing in place of another	**changeable** **changed** **changing**
channel	a narrow stretch of water between two pieces of land	
chapel	1. part of a large church used for special services 2. a small church, often in a college, hospital or school 3. churches of the Methodists and Baptists	
chapter	part of a book	
character	1. someone in a story or play 2. what a person is really like	
charge	1. to ask a certain price for something you are selling 2. to attack by rushing forward	**charged** **charging**
charm	1. a spell 2. to be pleasing to someone	**charmed** **charming**

chart	1. a piece of paper or card on which facts are displayed 2. a sea map	
chase	to run after	**chased** **chasing**
chat	to talk	**chatted** **chatting** **chatty**
chatter	to talk about unimportant things	**chatterbox** **chattered** **chattering**
chauffeur	someone who is paid to drive a car	
cheap	low in price	**cheaper** **cheapest** **cheaply**
cheat	to trick someone	**cheated** **cheating**
check	1. a squared pattern 2. to see if something is right 3. to stop or slow down	**checked** **checking**
cheek	1. the side of the face 2. rudeness	**cheeked** **cheeking** **cheeky**
cheer	1. to shout in joy 2. to make someone happy	**cheered** **cheerful** **cheerfully**
cheer up	to become happy	**cheering**
cheese	a food made from sour milk	
chemist	a person who prepares and sells medicines	**chemistry**
cherry	a small fruit which has a stone in the middle	**cherries**
chess	an indoor game played on a square board by two players	
chest	1. a large box 2. the upper front part of the body	
chestnut	a large tree; its nut is often called a conker	

chew	to bite with the teeth	**chewed** **chewing**
chicken	a young fowl	
chief	1. a leader: someone in charge 2. first in importance	**chiefly** **chieftain**
child	a young boy or girl	**children** **childish**
chill	1. a cold 2. cool	**chilly**
chime	1. the ringing of bells 2. to make a sound like a bell	**chimed** **chiming**
chimney	a flue for taking away smoke	
chimpanzee	a kind of monkey	
chin	the part of your face below the mouth	
china	cups, saucers and plates made from a fine clay	
chip	1. a thin slice of potato 2. to break off a small piece	**chipped** **chipping**
chisel	a sharp tool for cutting wood or stone	
chocolate	a sweet made from cocoa, milk and sugar	
choice	choosing from a number of things	
choir	a group of singers	
choke	to stop breathing by blocking the throat	**choked** **choking**
choose	to pick	**choosing** **chose** **chosen**
chop	1. a thick slice of meat containing a rib 2. to cut with an axe	**chopped** **chopping**
chopper	an axe	
chorus	1. a group of singers 2. the part of a song where everyone joins in	**choruses**
Christ	a name given to Jesus	

christen	to baptise and give a baby its Christian name	**christened** **christening**
Christian	a person who believes in Christ	
Christmas	the feast of the birthday of Jesus Christ	**Christmases**
chunk	a lump of something	
church	a building where Christians go to pray	**churches** **churchyard**
chute	a steep slide	
cider	a drink made from apple juice	
cigar	a roll of tobacco leaves for smoking	
cigarette	a small roll of tobacco, wrapped round with paper, for smoking	
cinder	a burnt piece of coal	
cinema	a place where films are shown	
circle	1. a perfectly round shape 2. to go round in a circle	**circled** **circling**
circumference	the distance round a circle	
circus	a travelling show with animals, acrobats and clowns	**circuses**
city	a large town	**cities**
claim	to demand something you have a right to	**claimed** **claiming**
clap	to slap your hands together	**clapped** **clapping**
clarinet	a musical wind instrument	
clash	a loud noise of things banging together	**clashes**
class	a group of people or things that are alike in some way	**classes** **classroom**
claw	the nails of an animal or bird	
clay	sticky earth that is used for making bricks or pottery	
clean	1. free from dirt 2. to take away the dirt from something	**cleaned** **cleaner** **cleanest** **cleaning** **cleanliness**

clear	1. easy to see or understand 2. to get rid of something	**cleared** **clearing** **clearly**
clergy	ministers who preach in church	
clerk	a person who works in an office	
clever	skilful or intelligent	**cleverly**
cliff	high, steep rock, usually at the edge of the sea	
climate	the weather	
climb	to go up, by using hands and feet	**climbed** **climber** **climbing**
cling	to hold on to	**clinging** **clung**
clinic	a building where you go to be examined or treated by a doctor	
clip	to cut with scissors or shears	**clipped** **clippers** **clipping**
cloak	a coat with no sleeves	
cloakroom	a place for leaving outdoor clothes	
clock	a machine for telling the time	**clockwise** **clockwork**
clog	1. a boot or shoe made of wood 2. to block	**clogged** **clogging**
close	1. near 2. very warm and stuffy 3. to shut	**closed** **closely** **closer** **closest** **closing**
cloth	material that is woven	**clothes** **clothing**

cloud	1. a cluster of very tiny drops of water floating in the sky	**cloudburst**
	2. a large amount of dust, smoke or steam	**clouded**
		clouding
		cloudless
		cloudy
clover	a small wild plant, used to feed cattle	
clown	a funny person, usually in a circus	
club	1. a stick with a thick, heavy end	
	2. a group of people who join together for some purpose	
clue	something that helps you to solve a problem	
clumsy	awkward in moving	**clumsier**
		clumsiest
		clumsily
clung	(The shipwrecked sailor *clung* to a piece of floating wood)	
coach	a carriage for carrying people by road or by rail	**coaches**
		coachman
coal	black fuel dug from the ground	
coarse	rough	
coast	where the sea meets the land	**coastguard**
coat	an outer covering	**coathanger**
cobbler	a shoe-mender	
cobweb	a spider's web	
cock	a male bird	
cockpit	where a pilot sits in an aircraft	
cocoa	powder made from cacao beans	
coconut	the fruit of the coco palm	
cod	a large fish caught for food	**cod**
code	a set of secret signs or letters	
coffee	a drink made from the roasted seed of a coffee tree	
coffin	the box in which a body is buried	

coil	rope or wire wound round and round	
coin	a piece of money	
coke	coal after the gas has been taken from it	
colander	a bowl with holes, for straining things	
cold	1. an illness of the nose and throat	
	2. not warm	colder coldest
collapse	to fall in a heap suddenly	collapsed collapsible collapsing
collar	a neck-band	
collect	to gather together	collected collecting collection collector
college	a school, usually for higher education	
collide	to bump together by mistake	collided colliding collision
colliery	a coal mine	collieries
colonel	an important officer in the army	
colour	1. (Red, blue and green are my favourite *colours*)	coloured colouring
	2. to paint or crayon	colourless
column	1. a line of troops	
	2. a pillar	
comb	1. (Peter used a *comb* to make his hair tidy)	combed combing
	2. (Jane went to *comb* her hair)	
come	to move towards	came coming
comedian	an actor who makes you laugh	
comfortable	at ease: contented	

comic	1. a paper for children	
	2. laughable	comical
comma	a sign used in writing, shaped like this ,	
command	1. an order	commanded
	2. to give orders	commander
		command-ing
commentator	someone who describes events on the radio or television	commentary
commercial	1. to do with trade	
	2. an advertisement on the radio or television	
committee	a group of people chosen to decide things	
common	1. an open space which anyone can use	
	2. happening often	
	3. vulgar	
compare	to see how things are different	compared comparing comparison
compass	a magnetised piece of iron or steel which always points to the north	compasses
compasses	a tool used for drawing circles	
competition	a game or sport held in order to find the winner	competitor
complain	to grumble about	complained complaining complaint
complete	1. whole	completed
	2. to finish	completely completing
composition	a written story	
computer	a machine for working out difficult problems with numbers	
concert	a musical entertainment	

CO

concrete	cement, sand, stones and water mixed together	
condition	the state something is in	
conduct	1. to guide 2. to direct an orchestra	conducted conducting conductor
cone	a solid shape with a round base tapering to a point	
confess	to own up	confessed confesses confessing confession
confetti	very small pieces of coloured paper, thrown at weddings	confetti
conjurer	a person who does clever tricks	conjuring
conker	the nut of the horse chestnut tree, used for playing the game of conkers	
connect	to join together	connected connecting connection connector
conquer	to defeat an enemy: to win	conquered conquering conqueror
conscious	knowing what is going on around you	
contain	to hold inside	contained container containing
content	happy: satisfied	contented
contest	a competition	
continent	a very large piece of land	continental
continue	to keep on	continually continued continuing continuous
contradict	to say that someone is wrong in something they have said	contradicted contradicting contradiction

control	1. to be in command of something 2. to hold in check	**controlled** **controlling**
convenient	easy: suitable	
convent	a house where nuns live	
conversation	talk	
convict	a person who has been sent to prison	
cook	1. someone who gets meals ready 2. to prepare food by heating	**cooked** **cookery** **cooking**
cool	1. slightly cold 2. to make anything less hot	**cooled** **cooler** **coolest** **cooling**
copper	a reddish metal	
copy	to imitate	**copied** **copies** **copying**
coral	a rock-like material made up of the skeletons of tiny sea creatures	
cord	strong string	
core	the part nearest the centre	
cork	1. the bark of a cork tree 2. a stopper made from cork	
corkscrew	a tool for taking a cork out of a bottle	
corn	grain used for food	**cornflakes**
corner	where two lines, or roads, meet	
cornet	1. a kind of trumpet 2. an ice-cream holder	
corpse	a dead body	
correct	1. right: exact: true 2. to put right	**corrected** **correcting** **correction** **correctly**
corridor	a passage-way	

cost	the price of something	**costly**
costume	dress	
cosy	1. a teapot cover	**cosies**
	2. comfortable and warm	
cottage	a small country house	
cotton	thread made from the cotton plant	
couch	a sofa	**couches**
cough	to force out air from the lungs suddenly and noisily	**coughed** **coughing**
could	(John *could* not come to school because he was ill)	
count	to see how many there are	**counted** **counting**
counter	1. the table in a shop over which you are served	
	2. a small disc used for playing some games, such as tiddly-winks	
country	1. a land where a nation of people lives	**countries** **country-**
	2. districts away from towns	**side**
county	part of a country	**counties**
couple	1. two: a pair	**coupled**
	2. to join together	**coupling**
coupon	a slip of paper which you can change for something else	
courage	boldness: bravery	**courageous**
course	1. (Of *course* I shall go to the party if I am asked)	
	2. a track for racing or for some types of games	
court	1. a closed-in space	**courtyard**
	2. the piece of ground on which some games such as tennis are played	
	3. a place where people are tried	
	4. the attendants of a king or queen	

cousin	a child of your uncle or aunt	
cover	to hide from view: to shelter	**covered** **covering**
coward	a person who has no courage	**cowardice** **cowardly**
cowboy	a person who lives on a ranch and looks after cattle	
crab	a sea animal which has a hard shell and strong claws	
crack	1. a sharp noise 2. to split	**cracked** **cracking**
cracker	1. an indoor firework 2. a sort of biscuit	
cradle	a cot for a baby	
crafty	artful: cunning	
cramp	a painful stiffness of the muscles	
crane	1. a machine for lifting heavy masses (weights) 2. a wading bird with long legs	
crash	the noise made when something bumps very sharply into something else	**crashes** **crashed** **crashes** **crashing**
crawl	1. to creep on the ground 2. to move slowly	**crawled** **crawling**
crayon	a coloured chalk or wax pencil	
craze	something which is very popular at the moment	
crazy	silly: mad	**crazily**
creak	to make a squeaking sound	**creaked** **creaking**
cream	the fatty part of milk that settles at the top	**creamy**
crease	1. a line made by folding 2. to fold and make a mark or line	**creased** **creasing**

create	to make	**created**
		creating
		creation
		creative
creature	a person, animal or insect	
creep	to move slowly and silently	**creeping**
		crept
crew	the people who work on a ship or aircraft	
cricket	1. a jumping insect that chirps	
	2. a summer game, in which a bat, ball and stumps are used	**cricketer**
cried	(The baby *cried* because she was hungry)	
crime	an evil deed	
criminal	someone who does a crime	
crimson	deep red	
crisp	1. a very thin slice of fried potato	
	2. hard but brittle	
crocodile	a large creature, shaped like a lizard, which lives in rivers in hot countries	
crocus	a plant that flowers early in the spring	**crocuses**
crook	1. a stick bent at the end in the shape of a hook	
	2. a thief	
crooked	not straight	
crop	1. the produce from a field or garden	
	2. to cut short	**cropped**
cross	1. anything shaped like the letter X	**crosses**
		crossed
	2. bad-tempered	**crosses**
	3. to go over from one side to the other	**crossing**

crouch	to stoop	**crouched** **crouches** **crouching**
crow	a large black bird	
crowd	a large number of people	**crowded** **crowding**
crown	1. the head-dress of a king or queen 2. to place a crown on some-one's head	**crowned** **crowning**
cruel	taking pleasure in causing pain	**cruelly** **cruelty**
cruet	a set of pots for salt, pepper and mustard	
crumb	a small piece of something like bread	
crumble	to break into small pieces	**crumbled** **crumbling**
crunch.	to crush with your teeth or under foot	**crunched** **crunches** **crunching**
crush	to squeeze very hard	**crushed** **crushes** **crushing**
crust	the hard outer covering	**crusty**
crutches	long sticks that lame people use to help them walk	
cry	1. a loud shout 2. to shout out 3. to shed tears	**cries** **cried** **cries** **crying**
cube	a solid shape with six square sides	**cubic**
cuckoo	a bird whose name comes from its call	
cucumber	a long, green-skinned vege-table	
cuddle	to put your arms round some-thing and hold it close	**cuddled** **cuddling** **cuddly**

cuff	the end of a coat or shirt sleeve	
culprit	the one who is to blame	
cunning	artful: crafty	
cupboard	space for storing things, with shelves and doors	
cure	to make better again	**cured** **curing**
curious	1. wanting to find out 2. strange	**curiosity** **curiously**
curl	1. anything that is twisted in-to ringlets 2. to twist into a curl	**curled** **curler** **curling** **curly**
currant	a dried grape	
current	a flow of water, air or elec-tricity	
curry	1. a strong tasting spice 2. a stew cooked with curry	
curtain	cloth hanging to form a screen	
curtsy	1. the way a lady bends her knees to give honour 2. to bend the knees in honour of someone	**curtsies** **curtsied** **curtsies** **curtsying**
curve	1. a smooth bend 2. to bend smoothly	**curved** **curving**
cushion	a soft loose pad used on a chair	
custard	eggs and milk mixed and cooked to form a pudding	
custom	what is usually done	
customer	a person who buys from a shop	
cut	to divide with something sharp	**cutter** **cutting**
cycle	to ride a bicycle	**cycled** **cycling** **cyclist**
cylinder	a tube-shaped object	**cylindrical**

d

daddy	a child's name for father	
daffodil	a yellow spring flower	
dagger	a short knife, sharp on both edges	
daily	every day	
dainty	neat: pretty: graceful	**daintily**
dairy	a place for keeping milk and cream, and for making butter	**dairies**
daisy	a small flower with white petals	**daisies**
damage	1. harm 2. to harm someone or something	**damaged** **damaging**
damp	slightly wet	
damson	a small plum	
dance	1. steps set to music 2. to move in time to music	**danced** **dancer** **dancing**
dandelion	a yellow wild flower	
danger	a risk: something which might be harmful	**dangerous** **dangerously**
dare	to be brave enough to do something	**dared** **daring**
dark	1. with little or no light 2. black, or nearly black	**darker** **darkest** **darkness**
darling	someone you love very much	
darn	to mend a hole by weaving cotton or wool over it	**darned** **darning**
dart	1. a short arrow 2. to move suddenly	**dartboard** **darted** **darting**
dash	1. a line like this — 2. to rush	**dashes** **dashed** **dashes** **dashing**

date	1. the fruit of a date palm tree 2. the day of the year you can read from a calendar
daughter	a girl child
dawdle	1. to idle or waste time **dawdled** 2. to walk slowly **dawdling**
dawn	the coming of daylight
day	1. twenty-four hours **daybreak** 2. the hours of daylight **daylight** **daytime**
dazed	not to know what you are doing: bewildered
dazzle	to be so bright as almost to **dazzled** blind anyone **dazzling**
dead	not living **deadly**
deaf	unable to hear **deafness**
deal	1. a bargain 2. an amount 3. to give out **dealer** 4. to do business with some- **dealing** one **dealt**
dear	1. high in price **dearer** 2. much loved **dearest**
death	the end of life
debt	something owed **debtor**
decay	1. damage caused by rotting **decayed** 2. to rot away **decaying**
December	the last month of the year
decent	respectable
decide	to make up your mind **decided** **deciding** **decision**
decimal	a tenth part
decimals	a way of counting in tens, tenths, hundredths, and so on
deck	the flat top part of a ship
declare	1. to say something very firmly **declared** 2. to close an innings at cricket **declaring**

decorate	1. to make something look beautiful 2. to give someone a medal	**decorated** **decorating** **decoration** **decorator**
deep	going a long way down	**deeper** **deepest** **deeply**
deer	a wild, four-legged animal, sometimes with horns	**deer**
defeat	to conquer	**defeated** **defeating**
defend	to protect	**defence** **defended** **defender** **defending**
define	to explain exactly	**defined** **defining** **definition**
definite	certain	**definitely**
defy	to refuse to obey someone	**defiance** **defied** **defies** **defying**
delay	1. to hold back 2. to put off	**delayed** **delaying**
deliberate	on purpose	**deliberately**
delicate	not strong: dainty	
delicious	very tasty	
delight	to please very much	**delighted** **delightful**
deliver	to hand on to someone else	**delivered** **delivering**
demand	to ask for something and insist upon it	**demanded** **demanding**
denominator	the number below the line in a fraction	
dense	thick	
dentist	a person who looks after people's teeth	

deny	to insist that something is not true	**denied** **denies** **denying**
depart	to leave	**departed** **departing** **departure**
department	one part of a big store or office	
depend	to rely on	**depended** **depending**
depot	a place where things are stored	
depth	how deep anything is	
describe	to say what a thing is like	**described** **describing** **description**
desert	1. land where nothing grows 2. to run away from someone or something	**deserted** **deserting**
deserve	to be worthy of	**deserved** **deserving**
design	a pattern or shape	
desk	a table used for reading or writing	
despair	1. hopelessness 2. to lose hope	**despaired** **despairing** **desperate**
destroy	to ruin completely	**destroyed** **destroyer** **destroying**
detective	someone who has the special job of finding criminals	
detergent	a powder or liquid used for cleaning	
devil	an evil spirit	
dew	small drops of water which form on things during the night	
diagonal	the line joining opposite corners of a rectangle	

diagram	a drawing made to explain something	
dial	1. the face of a clock 2. to ring a number on a tele-phone	**dialled** **dialling**
diameter	straight line across a circle, passing through the centre	
diamond	a precious stone	
diary	a notebook for keeping a record of daily happenings	**diaries**
dictation	writing down what is being said	
dictionary	a book of words and their meanings	**dictionaries**
die	to stop living	**dead** **died** **dying**
diesel	a special kind of engine which runs on oil fuel	
different	unlike: not the same	**difference** **differently**
difficult	hard to do	**difficulty**
dig	to turn over the ground	**digging** **dug**
dinghy	a small boat, often with sails	**dinghies**
dinner	the chief meal of the day	
direct	1. straight 2. to be in charge 3. to show or tell someone the way	**directed** **directing** **direction**
dirty	not clean	**dirtier** **dirtiest**
disagree	to differ: to argue: to quarrel	**disagreeable** **disagreed** **disagreeing** **disagree-ment**
disappear	to vanish from sight	**disappear-ance** **disappeared** **disappearing**

disappoint	to be not as good as expected	**dis-appointed** **disappoint-ing** **disappoint-ment**
disaster	a sudden or great misfortune	
disc	1. a flat, round shape 2. another name for a gramo-phone record	**discotheque**
discontented	not satisfied: unhappy	
discover	to find out	**discovered** **discovering**
discovery	something or some place that is found for the first time	**discoveries**
disease	illness	
disgrace	1. shame 2. to bring shame on anyone	**disgraced** **disgraceful** **disgracing**
disguise	1. something that changes a person's appearance so that you do not know him 2. to change the look of a person or thing	**disguised** **disguising**
disgust	disliking something very much	**disgusted** **disgusting**
dish	a shallow plate	**dishes**
dishonest	not truthful	**dishonesty**
dislike	not to like someone or some-thing	**disliked** **disliking**
dismiss	to send away	**dismissed** **dismisses** **dismissing**
disobey	not to do what you are told: to break rules	**dis-obedience** **disobedient** **disobeyed** **disobeying**
display	1. a show 2. to show	**displayed** **displaying**

disqualify	to put someone out of a game or race for not keeping to the rules	**disqualified**
dissolve	to vanish when stirred into a liquid	**dissolved** **dissolving**
distant	far away	**distance**
distinct	1. clear: plain 2. separate	**distinctly**
district	a part of a big area	
disturb	to unsettle or upset	**disturbance** **disturbed** **disturbing**
ditch	a long, narrow trench for draining water	**ditches**
dive	to go down head first	**dived** **diver** **diving**
divide	to separate into a number of parts	**divided** **dividing** **division**
dizzy	giddy	
dock	1. where a ship loads or unloads 2. where a prisoner stands in court 3. a weed	
doctor	someone who treats you when you are ill	
dodge	to get out of the way of	**dodged** **dodging**
does	(Jane *does* all her work neatly)	
doll	a toy baby or child	
dollar	an American coin	
dolphin	a sea animal like a porpoise	
done	finished	
donkey	an animal like a small horse with big ears	
door	an entrance to a room or building	

dope	to make someone sleep by giving him a drug	**doped** **doping**
dormouse	a small animal which hibernates	**dormice**
dose	the amount of medicine to be taken at a time	
double	1. twice as much 2. to fold over	**doubled** **doubling**
double-decker	a 'bus with seats upstairs as well as downstairs	
doubt	1. uncertainty 2. not to be certain	**doubted** **doubtful** **doubting**
dough	bread or pastry mixture before it is baked	**doughnut**
dove	a kind of pigeon	
down	1. soft feathers 2. from a higher to a lower place	**downward**
downpour	heavy rain	
downstairs	on a lower floor	
doze	to sleep lightly	**dozed** **dozing**
dozen	twelve	
drag	to pull along behind you	**dragged** **dragging**
dragon	a monster which was thought to breathe fire from its nostrils	
drain	1. a pipe for waste water 2. to empty 3. to dry something by taking the water away	**drainage** **drained** **draining**
drama	an exciting event, or play	
drank	(Tom *drank* to quench his thirst)	
draper	a person who sells goods made of cloth	

draught	1. a flow of air in a room	**draughty**
	2. a counter in the game of draughts	
draw	1. to pull along	**drawing**
	2. to make a picture of something	**drawn**
drawer	a sliding container in a piece of furniture	
dread	1. great fear	**dreaded**
	2. to fear a great deal	**dreadful**
		dreadfully
		dreading
dream	to have pictures in your mind while you are asleep	**dreamed**
		dreaming
		dreamt
		dreamy
drench	to wet all over	**drenched**
		drenches
		drenching
dress	1. clothing	**dresses**
	2. to put clothes on	**dressed**
		dresses
		dressing
drew	(Lisa *drew* a picture on the paper)	
dribble	1. to flow in drops	**dribbled**
	2. to move along with a football at your feet	**dribbling**
dried	(Anne *dried* herself with a towel)	
drift	1. snow heaped up by the wind	**drifted**
	2. to float along	**drifting**
drill	1. exercises which soldiers do	**drilled**
	2. to make a hole in something with a special tool	**drilling**
drink	to swallow liquid	**drank**
		drinking
		drunk
drip	to fall in drops	**dripped**
		dripping

drive
1. a private road, usually between a house and a public road
2. (Jill will *drive* a car when she is older) **driver** **driving**
3. to guide or chase animals **drove**

drizzle
1. misty rain **drizzled**
2. to rain very lightly **drizzling** **drizzly**

droop
to hang down in a tired way **drooped** **drooping**

drop
1. a small spot of liquid **dropped**
2. to fall or let fall **dropping**

drove
(He *drove* his car into the garage)

drown
to die under water because you cannot breathe **drowned** **drowning**

drug
1. a special sort of medicine **drugged**
2. to give someone a drug **drugging**

drum
a musical instrument made from stretched skin on a round frame **drummer**

drunk
1. (The man could not stand because he was *drunk*)
2. (I have *drunk* a glass of milk)

dry
1. without water **dried**
2. to take all the water away **drier** **dries** **drying**

duck
1. one of a group of birds that can swim
2. to move the head down sharply **ducked** **ducking**

duffel or **duffle-coat**
a jacket of coarse woollen material with a hood **duffle-bag**

dug
(I *dug* the garden with a spade)

dull
1. not bright or polished **duller**
2. slow to learn **dullest**

dumb
unable to speak

dump
1. a pile of rubbish **dumped**
2. to throw things in an un- **dumping** tidy heap

dungeon an underground prison

during while something is going on

dusk nightfall

dust
1. a fine powder in the air **dusted**
2. to remove dust **dusting**
dusty

dustbin a large container for rubbish

dustman someone who empties the **dustmen** dustbins

duty something that you should do **duties**

dwarf
1. a very small person **dwarfed**
2. small

dye to change the colour of some- **dyed** thing by dipping it in a special **dyeing** liquid

dying (The flowers were *dying* because they needed water)

dynamite a high explosive

dynamo a machine for making electricity

e

each every one

eager keen **eagerly**

eagle a bird of prey

ear part of the head with which **earache** you hear **earring**

early in good time: the opposite of **earlier** late **earliest**

earn to get something by working **earned** for it **earning**

earth   the ground: the world in which we live

earthquake   a shaking of the earth's surface

earwig   a small insect

easel   a three-legged wooden stand for a blackboard or picture

east   where the sun rises   **eastern**

Easter   the feast of the resurrection of Jesus Christ

easy   1. not difficult   **easier**
    2. comfortable   **easiest**
    easily

eat   to chew and swallow food   **ate**
    eatable
    eaten
    eating

echo   1. a sound coming back and heard a second time   **echoes**
    2. to make an echo   **echoed**
    echoes
    echoing

eclipse   a darkening of the sun when the moon passes between the earth and the sun

edge   the border

editor   a person who corrects a newspaper or book before it is printed

educate   to help people find out and learn: to teach   **educated**
    educating
    education

eel   a snake-like fish

effort   using strength to do something

eiderdown   a bed-cover, once stuffed with the feathers of an eider duck

eight   8   **eighth**

eighteen   18   **eighteenth**

eighty   80   **eightieth**

either   one or the other

elastic	a material which springs back to shape after it has been stretched	
elbow	the joint in the middle of the arm	
election	choosing by voting	
electric	worked by electricity	**electrical**
electricity	power that gives us light and heat	**electrician**
elephant	a huge animal, with a trunk and tusks	
eleven	11	**eleventh**
elf	a boy fairy	**elves**
elm	a large tree	
else	1. as well: besides 2. if not	**elsewhere**
embankment	a raised bank to carry a road or railway over low ground	
embroider	to decorate with coloured silks	**embroidered** **embroider-** **ing** **embroidery**
emerald	a precious green stone	
emigrate	to leave one country to go to live in another	**emigrated** **emigrating** **emigration**
empire	a number of countries ruled over by one government	**emperor** **empress**
employ	1. to use 2. to give work to: to keep busy	**employed** **employer** **employing** **employ-** **ment**
empty	1. containing nothing 2. to take everything out	**emptied** **empties** **emptying**
encourage	to help by praise or advice	**encouraged** **encourage-** **ment** **encouraging**

encyclopaedia   a book giving facts about many things

end   1. the finish of something
2. to finish
ended
ending
endless

enemy   someone who tries to harm you   **enemies**

engine   a machine for doing work   **engineer**

enjoy   to be pleased by something
enjoyable
enjoyed
enjoying
enjoyment

enormous   huge: very big
enough   as much as is needed

enquire   to ask about
enquired
enquiring
enquiry

enter   to go into
entered
entering
entry

entertain   to amuse
entertained
entertainer
entertaining
entertain-ment

entire   with no part missing: complete   **entirely**

entrance   the place where you go in
envelope   a paper cover for a letter
equal   exactly the same   **equally**

equator   an imaginary line marking the middle part of the earth, exactly halfway between the North and South Poles

equilateral   a figure or shape which has all its sides equal

erect   1. upright
2. to build
erected
erecting

errand   a short journey to take a message or collect something

escalator	a moving staircase	
escape	to get away from danger or something unpleasant	**escaped** **escaping**
especially	most of all	
essay	a composition: a written story	
estimate	to guess approximately what you think the answer will be	**estimated** **estimating** **estimation**
even	not odd: level: equal	**evenly**
evening	the end of the day	
event	something that happens	
eventually	at last: in the end	
ever	always: at all times	
evergreen	staying green all the year	
every	each one	**everybody** **everyone** **everything** **everywhere**
evil	wicked	
ewe	a female sheep	
exact	correct	**exactly**
exaggerate	to make something seem more than it is	**exaggerated** **exaggerat-ing** **exaggera-tion**
examine	1. to look at carefully 2. to test	**examina-tion** **examined** **examining**
example	a pattern: something to be copied	
excellent	very good indeed	
except	leaving out: but for	**exception**
exchange	1. a telephone switch-board 2. to change one thing for another	**exchanged** **exchanging**
excite	to thrill someone	**excited** **excitement** **exciting**

excursion	a pleasure trip	
excuse	1. a reason	**excused**
	2. to forgive	**excusing**
exercise	1. a practice	**exercised**
	2. to use your muscles by moving about	**exercising**
exhaust	1. the pipe that carries away waste fumes from an engine	**exhausted** **exhausting**
	2. to make tired	
exhibition	a display	
exist	to be	**existed** **existence** **existing**
exit	the way out	
expand	to get larger	**expanded** **expanding** **expanse**
expect	to look forward to	**expected** **expecting**
expedition	a journey by land or sea to discover things	
expel	to drive out: to turn out	**expelled** **expelling**
expense	the cost of something	**expensive**
experiment	a trial or a test	**experi- mental**
expert	someone who is very good in a certain job or subject	
explain	to make the meaning clear	**explained** **explaining** **explanation**
explode	to burst with a loud noise	**exploded** **exploding** **explosion** **explosive**
explore	to search	**exploration** **explored** **explorer** **exploring**
export	to send goods out of the country	**exported** **exporting**

express	1. a fast train	**expresses**
	2. to put into words or writing	**expressed**
		expresses
		expressing
extra	in addition	
extraordinary	out of the ordinary: very unusual	
eye	part of the head with which you see	**eyebrow**
		eyelash
		eyelid
		eyesight

f

fable	a story about animals, making them like real people	
face	1. the front part of your head	**faced**
	2. to turn your head towards	**facing**
fact	something that is true	
factor	a number that goes exactly into another number	**factorise**
factory	a building where things are made	**factories**
fade	1. to lose colour	**faded**
	2. to disappear slowly: to get weaker slowly	**fading**
fail	to try to do something and be unable to do it	**failed**
		failing
		failure
faint	1. not clear: dim: weak	**fainted**
	2. to lose your senses as if you were asleep	**fainting**
		faintly
fair	1. a collection of sideshows and roundabouts	**fairly**
	2. a big market	
	3. honest: just	
	4. beautiful	
	5. light-coloured	
	6. not very good	
	7. dry and sunny	

fairy	a small person in a story who does good by magic	**fairies** **fairyland** **fairytale**
faithful	trusting: reliable	**faithfully**
fake	something which is not what it is said to be	
fall	to tumble: to drop	**fallen** **falling** **fell**
false	1. not real 2. not true	
family	a group of people or things related to each other	**families**
famine	a very great shortage of food	
famished	very hungry	
famous	well known: important	
fancy	1. pretty: decorated 2. to imagine 3. to want	**fancied** **fancies** **fancying**
fare	the amount you pay to travel from one place to another	
farewell	goodbye	
farm	land which is tilled: land on which cattle are reared	**farmed** **farmhouse** **farming** **farmyard**
farmer	a person who looks after a farm	
farther	a longer way away	**farthest**
fast	1. quick: speedy 2. fixed tightly	**faster** **fastest**
fasten	1. to fix tightly 2. to join together	**fastened** **fastener** **fastening**
father	a male parent	
fault	1. a mistake 2. a failing	**faulty**
favour	a kindness	**favourite**
fawn	1. a yellowish-brown colour 2. a young deer	

fear	1. dread: terror	**feared**
	2. to be afraid of	**fearful**
		fearing
		fearless
		fearlessly
feast	a very special meal: a festival	**feasted**
		feasting
feather	(A bird's body is covered with	**feathered**
	feathers)	**feathery**
February	the second month of the year	
fed	(She *fed* her canary on bird seed)	
feeble	weak: dim	
feed	1. to give food to	**fed**
	2. to eat	**feeding**
feel	1. to touch	**feeling**
	2. to notice	**felt**
	3. to have feeling	
feet	(John's shoes pinched his *feet*)	
fell	(Rain *fell* and the match was stopped)	
fellow	a man or a boy	
felt	1. a thick woollen cloth	
	2. (I *felt* ill, so I stayed at home)	
female	a woman or a girl	
fence	a barrier round a garden or field to keep people out or animals in	**fencing**
fender	a metal guard to keep coals from falling from the fireplace	
fern	a plant with no flowers, found in woods	
ferret	a small thin animal that clears rabbits out of their holes	
ferry	a boat that travels backwards and forwards over a narrow stretch of water	**ferries**
festival	a time for merry-making	

fetch	to go for something and bring it back	**fetched** **fetches** **fetching**
fever	an illness that makes you feel hot	**feverish**
fibre	a small thread of something	
fiction	a story that is made up	
fiddle	1. another word for violin	
	2. to play idly with something	**fiddled** **fiddling**
fidget	to move restlessly	**fidgeted** **fidgeting** **fidgety**
field	1. a piece of land with a hedge or fence round it	
	2. to catch, stop or throw the ball at cricket	**fielded** **fielder** **fielding**
fierce	savage: cruel	**fiercely**
fifteen	15	**fifteenth**
fifth	5th	
fifty	50	**fiftieth**
fight	1. a struggle	**fighting**
	2. to struggle with	**fought**
figure	a number	
file	1. a tool for smoothing things	**filed**
	2. a line of people one behind another	**filing**
	3. to use a file	
fill	to make full	**filled** **filling**
film	1. a moving picture shown on a screen	**filmed** **filming**
	2. a roll put in a camera for taking photographs	
	3. a thin skin	
	4. to take a moving picture of something	
filter	material for straining liquids	
filthy	dirty: foul	

final	the last: at the very end	**finalist** **finally**
find	to discover: to come across	**finding** **found**
fine	1. money to be paid as a punishment for something you have done wrong	**fined**
	2. sunny	**finer**
	3. thin	**finest**
	4. excellent	
finger	(I have four *fingers* and one thumb on each hand)	**finger-nail** **finger-print**
finish	to end: to complete	**finished** **finishes** **finishing**
fir	a tall evergreen tree	
fire	1. when something burns	**fired**
	2. to shoot with a gun	**firing**
firefighter	a person whose job it is to put out fires	
fireplace	the place in a room where the fire burns	
fireside	the place near a fire	
firewood	wood used for lighting a fire	
fireworks	(We let off *fireworks* on November 5th each year)	
firm	1. a business	
	2. strong: steady	**firmly**
first	at the beginning: with nothing in front	**firstly**
fish	1. one of a group of animals that live in water	**fish** or **fishes**
	2. to try to catch fish	**fished** **fishes** **fishing**
fisherman	someone who catches fish	**fishermen**
fishmonger	someone who sells fish	
fist	a tightly closed hand	

fi fl

fit	1. healthy 2. to be the right size	**fitted** **fitter** **fittest** **fitting**
five	5	**fifth**
fix	1. trouble 2. to fasten 3. to arrange	**fixed** **fixes** **fixing**
fixture	a match or game arranged against another team	
flag	a banner on a stick or pole	
flake	a small, thin, light piece	
flame	1. the blaze of a fire 2. to burn like a flame	**flamed** **flaming**
flannel	1. smooth cloth made of wool 2. face-cloth	
flap	to move like wings	**flapped** **flapping**
flare	to throw out flames suddenly	**flared** **flaring**
flash	1. a light that suddenly comes and goes 2. to come and go very quickly	**flashes** **flashed** **flashes** **flashing**
flask	a small bottle with a narrow neck	
flat	1. a set of rooms on one floor 2. level and smooth 3. below the note in music	**flatter** **flattest**
flatten	to make flat	**flattened** **flattening**
flavour	1. the taste of anything 2. to make tasty	**flavoured** **flavouring**
flea	a tiny, jumping insect that bites	
fled	ran away	
fleet	a group of ships, lorries or buses	

flesh	the soft part of the body, under the skin	**fleshy**
flew	(The bird *flew* high into the air)	
flick	to hit something lightly	**flicked** **flicking**
flicker	to burn shakily	**flickered** **flickering**
flies	(An owl usually *flies* at night)	
flight	a journey by air	
fling	to throw hard	**flinging** **flung**
flint	a very hard kind of rock	
float	to rest on, or near, the top of water	**floated** **floating**
flock	a number of birds or animals together	
flood	1. an overflow of water from a a river or the sea 2. to overfill with liquid	**flooded** **flooding** **floodlight**
floor	the part of a room on which you walk	
flour	corn ground to powder	
flow	to move along smoothly	**flowed** **flowing**
flower	a blossom on a plant	**flowery**
'flu	short way of writing influenza	
fluff	soft, feathery stuff	**fluffy**
flung	(He *flung* the ball at the wicket)	
flute	a musical wind instrument	
fly	1. a small winged insect 2. to move through the air	**flies** **flew** **flies** **flown** **flying**
foam	1. froth 2. to make foam	**foamed** **foaming**
foggy	very misty	**foggier** **foggiest**

fold	1. a crease	**folded**
	2. a fenced area in which sheep are kept	**folding**
	3. to crease: to bend over	
folder	a cover in which to keep papers	
follow	1. to come after: to go behind	**followed**
	2. to understand	**follower**
		following
fond	loving	**fondly**
food	anything to eat or drink	
fool	1. a very silly person	**fooled**
	2. to make someone believe something that is not true	**fooling**
		foolish
		foolishly
foot	1. the lowest part of the leg	
	2. the lowest part of anything	
	3. a measure of length	
football	a winter game played with a large leather ball	**footballer**
footpath	a narrow path to walk on	
footprint	the mark left by a foot	
footstep	the sound of a step	
forbid	to tell someone that they must not do something	**forbade**
		forbidden
		forbidding
force	1. strength	
	2. to make someone do something against his will	**forced**
		forcing
forecast	to say what will happen	**forecasting**
forehead	the part of the head just above the eyes	
foreign	belonging to another land	**foreigner**
foreman	a supervisor in charge of some workers	**foremen**
forest	a large area of trees	
forget	1. to put out of your mind	**forgetful**
	2. not to be able to remember	**forgetting**
		forgot
		forgotten

forgive	to pardon: to stop being cross with someone	**forgave** **forgiven** **forgiveness** **forgiving**
fork	1. a pronged tool for lifting earth or food 2. where a road divides in two	**forked**
form	1. the shape 2. a class 3. a bench 4. questions on a paper with blank spaces for the answers 5. to make	**formed** **forming**
fort	a castle, or strong building, which can be defended	**fortress**
fortnight	two weeks	
fortune	1. luck 2. wealth	**fortunate** **fortunately**
forty	40	**fortieth**
forward	to the front: onwards	
fossil	the remains or print of an ancient animal or plant, found in rock	
fought	(The boxer *fought* hard, but was beaten)	
foul	1. dirty: filthy 2. not to keep to the rules of the game	**fouled** **fouling**
found	(I lost my watch but *found* it the next day)	
fountain	a jet of water shooting upwards	
four	4	**fourth**
fourteen	14	**fourteenth**
fowl	a cock or hen	**fowl**
fox	a sly, wild animal like a dog	**foxes**
fraction	a part of anything	
frame	1. the border round a picture 2. the supports around which something is built	

freckle	a small brown spot on the skin	**freckled**
free	1. able to do as you like	**freed**
	2. loose	**freeing**
	3. not costing anything	**freely**
freedom	being free	
freeze	1. to turn water into ice	**freezing**
	2. to be very cold	**froze**
		frozen
fresh	1. new	**freshly**
	2. clean and pure	
	3. not feeling tired	
Friday	the sixth day of the week	
fried	(My father *fried* the fish)	
friend	someone you are fond of	**friendly**
		friendship
frieze	a border or strip of pictures on a wall	
fright	fear: terror	**frighten**
		frightened
		frightening
		frightful
frill	a wavy edge on anything	**frilled**
		frilly
fringe	short hair combed down over the forehead	
frisky	lively	
frock	a dress	
frog	a small animal that jumps and lives in and out of water	
from	out of	
front	the forward part	
frost	frozen dew or mist	**frosty**
froth	lots of air bubbles on top of a liquid	**frothed**
		frothing
		frothy
frown	to draw the eye-brows together	**frowned**
		frowning

frozen	1. turned to ice 2. stiff with cold	
fruit	the part of a plant which is sometimes eaten and which has seeds inside	
fry	to cook in boiling fat or oil	**fried** **fries** **frying**
fuel	anything used to make heat or power	
full	filled so that no more can go in	**fully**
fumble	to be clumsy in handling something	**fumbled** **fumbling**
fumes	smoke, gas or steam	
fund	money collected for a special reason	
funeral	a burial service	
funnel	1. the chimney of a ship 2. a tube with a wide mouth for pouring liquids	
funny	comical	**funnier** **funniest**
fur	the hair and skin of an animal	**furry**
furnace	a closed fireplace where a very hot fire can be made	
furnish	to fit up a house with tables, chairs, beds and other things	**furnished** **furnishes** **furnishing** **furniture**
furrow	a trench made by a plough	
further	1. a longer way away 2. more 3. in addition	**furthest**
fury	anger: rage	**furious** **furiously**
fuse	a safety wire that melts if the electric wires joined to it become too hot	**fused** **fusing**
fuselage	the body of an aircraft	

fuss	to worry about things that do not matter	**fussy**
future	the time which has yet to come	

g

gag	1. something put over some- one's mouth so that he can- not talk 2. to stop up someone's mouth	**gagged** **gagging**
gaily	merrily: happily	
gain	to get: obtain	**gained** **gaining**
gale	a very strong wind	
gallon	eight pints	
gallop	to run in leaps, as a horse does	**galloped** **galloping**
game	1. a sport 2. animals or birds that are hunted	
gander	a male goose	
gang	a group of people who work together	**gangster**
garage	a place where cars are re- paired or where they are kept	
garden	land used for growing flowers, fruit and vegetables	**gardener** **gardening**
gas	1. a fuel 2. anything, such as air, which is neither solid nor liquid	
gate	a door in a fence or wall	
gather	to collect together	**gathered** **gathering**
gave	(Sarah *gave* her sister some of her marbles)	

gaze	to stare at	**gazed** **gazing**
gazelle	a small antelope	
geese	the plural of goose	
general	1. a very important officer in the army	
	2. usual	**generally**
generous	not mean: ready to help any-one	**generously**
gentle	quiet: kind	**gently**
gentleman	a man who is well-mannered	**gentlemen**
geography	the study of people, places and things	
germ	a living thing which is too small to be seen without a magnifying glass but which may make you ill	
get	1. to obtain: to receive	**getting**
	2. to become	**got**
ghost	1. something imagined but not real	**ghostly**
	2. the soul of a person who is dead	
giant	a very large person or thing	
giddy	dizzy	**giddier** **giddiest** **giddiness**
gift	a present: something given	
ginger	1. a reddish-yellow colour	
	2. the root of a plant which tastes very hot	**gingerbread**
gipsy	one of a type of dark-skinned people who wander from place to place	**gipsies**
giraffe	an animal with very long legs and neck	
girl	a female child	
give	to hand over something	**gave** **given** **giving**

glacier	a slow-moving river of ice	
glad	pleased	**gladly**
glance	1. a quick look	**glanced**
	2. to look quickly at something	**glancing**
glance off	to bounce off	
glare	1. to stare fiercely	**glared**
	2. to shine brightly and dazzle	**glaring**
glass	1. the stuff from which window-panes are made	
	2. a drinking cup made of glass	**glasses**
	3. a mirror	
glasses	a pair of spectacles	
glide	to move smoothly and quietly	**glided**
		gliding
glider	an aeroplane with no engine	
glimpse	a quick look at something	
glitter	to sparkle	**glittered**
		glittering
globe	1. a ball-shape	
	2. a map of the earth in the shape of a ball	
gloomy	1. dark	
	2. miserable	
glorious	splendid: magnificent	
glove	a covering for the hand	
glow	to burn brightly without flames	**glowed**
		glowing
glue	sticky stuff for joining things together	
glum	sad: gloomy	
gnat	a small mosquito or fly that bites	
gnaw	to keep biting something and so wear it away	**gnawed**
		gnawing
gnome	a dwarf who is supposed to live under the ground	

go	to move	**goes** **going** **gone**
goal	1. something to be aimed at 2. a target in a game	**goalkeeper** **goalmouth** **goalpost**
goat	a small animal with horns which is useful for its milk and hair	
gobble	to eat quickly and noisily	**gobbled** **gobbling**
goblin	an ugly elf who is full of mischief	
god	one who is worshipped	
godfather	a man who makes promises for a baby at its christening	
godmother	a woman who makes promises for a baby at its christening	
godparent	a godfather or godmother	
going	(We are *going* to the seaside in the summer)	
gold	a precious yellow metal	**golden**
gone	(My friend has *gone* away)	
good	1. well-behaved 2. above average 3. suitable	**goodness**
goodbye	(Before leaving we said *goodbye*)	
goose	a large bird with a long neck and webbed feet	**geese**
gooseberry	a small hairy green fruit	**gooseberries**
gorge	a narrow strip of land with cliffs or mountains on either side	
gorgeous	beautifully coloured	
gorilla	the largest kind of ape	

go gr

gorse	a prickly bush with yellow flowers	
govern	to rule over	**governed** **governing** **government** **governor**
grab	to snatch	**grabbed** **grabbing**
grace	1. charm: beauty 2. a prayer before or after meals	**gracious**
graceful	full of charm: moving beautifully and easily	**gracefully**
gradually	little by little	
grain	1. corn 2. a very small piece of anything 3. the pattern in a piece of wood	
gramophone	a machine that plays records, an old-fashioned record-player	
gramme	a measure of mass (weight) in the metric system	
grand	splendid: important	
grandchild	the child of a person's son or daughter	**grandchildren**
grandfather	the father of a person's mother or father	
grandmother	the mother of a person's mother or father	
grandson	the son of a person's son or daughter	
granite	a very hard rock	
granny	grandmother	**grannies**
grape	the fruit of the vine plant	
grapefruit	a pale yellow fruit like a large orange	
graph	a diagram giving mathematical information, usually drawn on squared paper	

grasp	1. a firm grip	**grasped**
	2. to take hold of	**grasping**
grass	plants with thin green leaves grown as lawns and in fields	**grass** or **grasses**
grasshopper	a small jumping insect	
grate	a part of a fireplace	
grateful	thankful	**gratefully**
grave	1. a burial place	**gravely**
	2. solemn: serious	**gravestone**
		graveyard
gravity	the force that pulls things towards the centre of the earth	
gravy	the juice that comes from meat when it is cooked	
graze	1. to feed on grass in a field	**grazed**
	2. to scrape the skin	**grazing**
grease	1. thick fat or oil	**greased**
	2. to put grease on something	**greasing** **greasy**
great	large: important	**greater** **greatest** **greatly**
greedy	wanting more than is good for you	**greedier** **greediest** **greedily** **greediness**
green	the colour of grass	
greengrocer	someone who sells fruit and vegetables	
greenhouse	a glass house for plants	
greet	to welcome	**greeted** **greeting**
grew	(The seed *grew* into a beautiful plant)	
grey	the colour of a rainy sky	**greyish**
greyhound	a long-legged dog that runs very fast	
grin	1. a broad smile	**grinned**
	2. to give a broad smile	**grinning**

grind	1. to crush to powder	**grinding**
	2. to sharpen	**ground**
grip	1. a tight hold	**gripped**
	2. to hold tightly	**gripping**
gristle	the tough, stringy part of meat	**gristly**
grit	small bits of sand or stone	**gritty**
groan	1. a deep, slow sound made in pain, or when you are sad	**groaned** **groaning**
	2. to moan in pain or sadness	
grocer	someone who sells most kinds of dry or tinned foods	
grocery	what you buy from the grocer	**groceries**
ground	1. the earth	
	2. crushed to powder	
group	a number of people or things	
grouse	1. a moorland bird	**grouse**
	2. a grumble	**groused**
	3. to complain or grumble	**grousing**
grow	1. to get larger	**grew**
	2. to produce	**growing**
	3. to become	**grown**
		growth
growl	the sound a dog makes when it is disturbed	**growled** **growling**
grub	a caterpillar or a maggot	
grubby	dirty and untidy	
grumble	to complain	**grumbled** **grumbling**
grunt	to make a short pig-like noise	**grunted** **grunting**
guard	to look after: to keep safe	**guarded** **guarding**
guess	to say something without being sure	**guessed** **guesses** **guessing**
guide	1. a person who shows the way	**guided** **guiding**
	2. to show the way	

guilty	having done something wrong
guinea-pig	a small animal kept as a pet
guitar	a musical instrument with six strings
gum	1. the part of your mouth in which your teeth grow
	2. a thick liquid for sticking **gummed** things together　　　　　**gumming**
	3. to stick with gum
gunpowder	powder used for blowing things up
gust	a sudden rush of wind　　　　**gusty**
gutter	the edge of a road or roof along which water can run away
guy	a doll dressed up and meant to be like Guy Fawkes
gymnasium	a room for physical training
gypsy	one of a type of people who **gypsies** travel from place to place

h

habit	custom: anything you do regu-　**habitual** larly
haddock	a fish which belongs to the　**haddock** cod family of fish
hail	frozen rain
hair	it grows on people's heads　**hair-cut** and on some animals' bodies　**hairdresser** **hairy**
half	one of the parts of something　**halves** divided in two
halfpenny	two of them make one penny　**halfpennies**

hall	1. a large room in a building where people can gather together 2. the front passage in a house	
halo	a ring of light	**haloes**
halt	to come to a stop	**halted** **halting**
halve	to divide into two parts, both the same size	**halved** **halves** **halving**
hammer	1. a tool with a heavy head for knocking things 2. to use a hammer	**hammered** **hammering**
hamster	an animal like a large mouse	
hand	1. the part of the body at the end of the arm 2. to pass something to some-one	**handed** **handful** **handing**
handcuffs	a pair of steel rings put round a prisoner's wrists	
handkerchief	a piece of cloth for wiping your nose	
handle	1. the part of anything for holding 2. to hold with your hands	**handled** **handling**
handle-bar	the bar across a bicycle which you hold to guide it	
handsome	good-looking	
handwriting	words written by hand	
handy	1. useful 2. nearby 3. clever with your hands	**handier** **handiest**
hang	to fasten anything so that it can swing	**hanged** **hanging** **hung**
hangar	a shed for aeroplanes	
happen	to take place	**happened** **happening**

happy	pleased: joyful	**happier** **happiest** **happily** **happiness**
harbour	a place where ships can shelter	
hard	1. tough and solid 2. difficult 3. strict	
hardly	only just	
hare	an animal that is like a large rabbit	
harm	1. damage: hurt 2. to damage or hurt	**harmed** **harmful** **harming**
harpoon	a spear for killing whales	
harvest	1. crops gathered in 2. the time for gathering in crops 3. to gather in crops	**harvested** **harvester** **harvesting**
haste	hurry: speed	**hasten** **hasty**
hat	a covering for the head	
hatch	1. an opening in a wall, floor, roof or ship's deck 2. to be born from an egg	**hatches** **hatched** **hatches** **hatching** **hatchway**
hate	to dislike a great deal	**hated** **hateful** **hating** **hatred**
haunted	visited by ghosts	
have	to own: to hold	**had** **having**
hayrick **haystack**	a large neat pile of hay	
haze	a light mist	**hazy**
hazel	a small tree which sometimes produces nuts	

he

head	1. the top of the body	**headed**
	2. the top part of anything	**headfirst**
	3. the most important	**heading**
	4. to knock a ball with your	**head-**
	head	**quarters**
headache	a pain in the head	
headlight	one of the main lights on the front of a car	
headlong	rashly, without thought	
headmaster	the chief master in a school	
headmistress	the chief mistress in a	**head-**
	school	**mistresses**
heal	to cure: to get better	**healed**
		healing
health	the state your body is in when	**healthier**
	it is fit	**healthiest**
		healthy
heap	1. a pile	**heaped**
	2. to pile things up	**heaping**
hear	to listen to, or get word from	**heard**
	someone	**hearing**
heart	1. the part of the body that	**heartbeat**
	pumps blood	**heartfelt**
	2. the centre of anything	**hearty**
heat	1. warmth	**heated**
	2. to warm anything	**heating**
heath	moorland: waste land with grass and heather growing on it	
heather	a plant that grows on heaths	
heaven	the kingdom of God	**heavenly**
heavy	having a lot of mass (weight)	**heavier**
		heaviest
		heavily
hedge	a border made of shrubs or bushes which acts as a fence	
hedgehog	a small animal with a prickly back	

heel	the back part of the foot or shoe	**heeled**
heel over	to tilt: to lean	
height	how tall a thing is	
held	(The guard *held* up her flag)	
helicopter	an aircraft that has a propeller on the top and can fly straight upwards	
helmet	a very strong covering to protect the head	
help	1. assistance: aid 2. to assist: to aid	**helped** **helpful** **helpfully** **helping** **helpless** **helplessly**
hem	1. the edge of a piece of cloth turned over and stitched 2. to turn over and stitch the edge of a piece of cloth	**hemmed** **hemming**
herd	a number of animals together	
here	in this place	
hero	a very brave man or boy	**heroes** **heroic**
heroine	a very brave woman or girl	
herring	a small sea fish caught for food	
herself	she	
hesitate	to wait for a moment before doing something	**hesitated** **hesitating** **hesitation**
hexagon	a flat shape with six sides	
hibernate	to sleep all through the winter	**hibernated** **hibernating** **hibernation**
hide	1. the skin of an animal 2. to put out of sight	**hid** **hidden** **hiding**

high	tall: far up	**higher**
		highest
		highly
highway	a road	
highwayman	a highway robber	**highwaymen**
hi-jack	to force a pilot of an aircraft to	**hi-jacked**
	change course	**hi-jacking**
hike	to walk a long distance, usu-	**hiked**
	ally on holiday	**hiker**
		hiking
hill	a small mountain	**hilly**
himself	he	
hinder	to delay or prevent	**hindered**
		hindering
		hindrance
hinge	a joint on which a door or lid	
	swings	
hippopotamus	a large, heavy animal that	**hippopota-**
	lives in water and on land	**muses**
hire	to pay for the use of some-	**hired**
	thing	**hiring**
history	the subject that tells of people	**historical**
	or things of the past	
hitch-hike	to ask for a free lift in a car or	**hitch-hiked**
	lorry	**hitch-hiking**
hive	a home for bees making honey	
hoard	1. a store of things hidden	**hoarded**
	away	**hoarding**
	2. to store things up in secret	
hoarse	rough sounding: husky	
hobble	to walk awkwardly, as when	**hobbled**
	you are lame	**hobbling**
hobby	a pastime	**hobbies**
hockey	a game played with bent sticks	
	and a small ball	
hold	1. the part of the ship where	
	the cargo is stored	
	2. to take in your hands	**held**
	3. to contain	**holder**
		holding

hole	an opening: a hollow	
holiday	a time for doing what you like	
hollow	1. a hole 2. empty	
holly	an evergreen bush with red berries and prickly leaves	
hollyhock	a tall plant with large flowers	
holster	a holder for a revolver	
holy	pure: without sin	**holier** **holiest** **holiness**
home	where anyone lives	**homeless** **homely** **homesick** **homeward** **homework**
honest	truthful	**honestly** **honesty**
honey	the sweet syrup that bees make	
honeysuckle	a climbing plant with a sweet-smelling flower	
honour	1. glory 2. to praise or respect	**honoured** **honouring**
hood	a covering for the head and neck	**hooded**
hoof	the bottom part of some animal's feet	**hooves**
hook	a curved piece of metal	**hooked** **hooking**
hooligan	a rough, badly-behaved person	
hoop	a large wooden or metal ring	
hoot	to make a sound like an owl	**hooted** **hooter** **hooting**
hop	1. a plant used for making beer 2. to jump along on one foot	**hopped** **hopping**

hope	to wish for something to come true	**hoped** **hopeful** **hopefully** **hopeless** **hopelessly** **hoping**
horizon	where the sky seems to meet the land	**horizontal**
horn	1. a curved bone covered with hard skin sticking out of an animal's head 2. a musical wind instrument	
horrible	awful: dreadful	**horribly**
horrid	frightful: horrible	**horridly**
horrified	shocked	
horror	dread: great fear	
horse	a large animal used for riding or pulling loads	**horseshoe**
hose	a long rubber or plastic pipe	**hosepipe**
hospital	a building where sick people are looked after	
hot	very warm	**hotly** **hotter** **hottest**
hotel	a place where people pay to sleep and eat	
hound	a dog used in hunting	
hour	sixty minutes	**hourly**
house	a building in which a family lives	**household** **housekeeper** **housekeep-** **ing** **housing**
hover	to stay in the air over a place	
hovercraft	a cross between a ship and an aircraft, which hovers just above the surface	**hovercraft**
howl	1. a long, loud cry, like that of a dog 2. to cry out like a dog	**howled** **howling**

huddle	to get close together	**huddled** **huddling**
hug	to put your arms round	**hugged** **hugging**
huge	very large	
hum	to make a sound like a bee	**hummed** **humming**
hump	a lump on the back	**humped**
hundred	100	**hundredth**
hundredweight	one hundred and twelve pounds	
hung	(Jim *hung* his cap on the peg)	
hunger	the need for food	**hungrier** **hungriest** **hungrily** **hungry**
hunt	to try to catch wild animals	**hunted** **hunting**
hunt for	to search for	**hunter** **hunting** **huntsman**
hurrah	a shout of joy	
hurricane	a very strong wind	
hurry	to go quickly	**hurried** **hurries** **hurrying**
hurt	to harm: to damage	**hurting**
husband	a man who has a wife	
hush	silence	
hutch	a cage for rabbits	**hutches**
hyacinth	a sweet-smelling spring flower	
hyena	a wild animal like a dog, that lives in Africa or Asia	
hymn	a song of praise	

i

ice	frozen water	iceberg ice-cream iced icing icy
icicle	ice that hangs like a spike	
idea	a thought	
idiot	a fool	
idle	doing nothing	idled idleness idling idly
igloo	an Inuit ice-house	
ill	1. not well 2. evil	illness
imagine	to make a picture of some-thing in your mind	imagination imagined imagining
imitate	to do the same as someone else	imitated imitating imitation
immediately	straight away	
impatient	not willing to wait: restless	impatience
import	to bring goods into the coun-try	imported importing
important	worth thinking about or look-ing at	importance
impossible	cannot be done	impossibility
improve	to make, or to get, better	improved improve- ment improving
inch	twelve of them make a foot	inches
include	to put with other things in a a group	included including
increase	1. to get bigger 2. to make bigger	increased increasing

indeed	really	
index	alphabetical list showing where to find things in a book	
indoors	in a house or building	
infant	a very young child	
influenza	a feverish cold	
inform	to tell someone about something	**information** **informed** **informing**
injure	to hurt in some way	**injured** **injuring** **injury**
ink	used with a pen for writing	**inkwell** **inky**
inland	away from the sea	
innings	the time spent batting by a team or one player	
innocent	not guilty	
inquire	to ask about	**inquired** **inquiring** **inquiry**
insect	a small creature	
inside	within	
insist	to be very firm in saying something	**insisted** **insisting**
insolent	rude: cheeky	**insolence**
inspect	to look at closely for faults	**inspected** **inspecting** **inspection** **inspector**
instalment	one part of a story or payment	
instant	a very short space of time	**instantly**
instead	in place of	
instrument	1. a special tool 2. anything with which music is made	
intelligent	quick at learning	**intelligence**
intend	to be going to do something	**intended** **intending** **intention**

interest	1. curiosity 2. what people charge you if they lend you money 3. to hold your attention	**interested** **interesting**
interfere	1. to meddle 2. to get in the way	**interfered** **interference** **interfering**
interrupt	to stop someone when he is talking or working	**interrupted** **interrupting** **interruption**
interval	1. the space between 2. a rest	
into	right in	
introduce	1. to bring in 2. to bring two people to-gether	**introduced** **introducing** **introduction**
invade	to enter another country in order to conquer it	**invaded** **invading** **invasion**
invalid	a person who is not well	
invent	to make for the first time	**invented** **inventing** **invention** **inventor**
investigate	to examine very carefully	**investigated** **investigat-ing** **investiga-tion**
invisible	unable to be seen	
invite	to ask someone to come	**invitation** **invited** **inviting**
iron	1. a hard metal 2. a tool for smoothing cloth 3. to smooth with an iron	**ironed** **ironing**
ironmonger	a person who sells iron goods	
island	land surrounded by water	
isosceles	a triangle with two of its sides equal is called an isosceles triangle	

itch	1. a tickling on your skin	**itches**
	2. to feel a tickling on your skin	**itched**
		itches
		itching
itself	it	
ivory	the material elephants' tusks are made of	
ivy	an evergreen climbing plant	

j

jab	to poke in a rough way	**jabbed**
		jabbing
jack	a tool for raising heavy things	
jackal	a wild animal like a dog	
jackdaw	the smallest bird of the crow family	
jacket	a short coat	
jagged	rough at the edge	
jaguar	a fast-running wild animal	
jail	1. a prison	**jailer**
	2. to put a person in prison	
jam	1. fruit boiled with sugar	
	2. to become packed tightly	**jammed**
		jamming
January	the first month of the year	
jaw	the lower part of the face	
jazz	lively music with a strong rhythm	
jealous	envious	**jealousy**
jeans	tight trousers made from a material like thin canvas	
jeep	a small truck which can travel over rough ground and which has a very powerful engine	
jelly	fruit or meat juice that has set stiff	**jellies**

jellyfish	a fish like a floating piece of jelly	**jellyfish** or **jellyfishes**
jerk	to move something suddenly	**jerked** **jerking** **jerky**
jersey	a long-sleeved pullover	
jet	a thin stream of liquid or gas forced out through a pipe	**jet-propelled**
jetty	a small pier	**jetties**
jewel	a precious stone	**jewelled** **jeweller** **jewellery**
jig-saw	a picture cut into pieces that can be fitted together	
job	the work a person does	
jockey	a person who rides racehorses	
jog	1. to push with the elbow or hand 2. to trot in a tired way	**jogged** **jogging**
join	1. to fix things together 2. to become a member of	**joined** **joining**
joint	1. a piece of meat 2. a place where parts of something are joined	**jointed**
joke	1. something said or done that is funny 2. to make a joke	**joked** **joker** **joking**
jolly	happy: merry	**jollier** **jolliest**
journalist	someone who writes for a newspaper or magazine	
journey	going from one place to another	
joy	happiness: gladness	**joyful** **joyfully**
judge	1. someone who hears both sides of an argument, and then decides which is right 2. to decide: to give an opinion about something	**judged** **judgement** **judging**

juggler	a person who does throwing and catching tricks	
juice	the liquid from fruit	**juicy**
July	the seventh month of the year	
jumble	1. a number of things mixed up 2. to mix up	**jumbled** **jumbling**
jump	to spring: to leap	**jumped** **jumping**
jumper	a blouse made of wool	
June	the sixth month of the year	
jungle	a forest of thickly twined trees, plants and bushes, in hot lands	
junior	a younger person: younger	
junk	1. rubbish 2. a Chinese sailing boat	
jury	a group of people who decide whether someone is guilty or not	**juries**
just	1. fair 2. exactly: at this very minute	
justice	fairness	

k

kangaroo	an Australian animal with long back legs, which moves by jumping	
kayak	an Inuit canoe	
keel	a length of wood or metal on which a boat is built, and which stops it turning over	
keen	1. eager 2. sharp	**keener** **keenest** **keenly**

ke ki

keep	1. part of a castle 2. to take care of 3. to own something 4. to stay fresh 5. to continue	**keeper** **keeping** **kept**
kennel	a house for a dog	
kept	(He *kept* his coat on because it was cold)	
kerb	the stone edge of a path or pavement	**kerbstone**
ketchup	sauce made from vegetables	
kettle	a container made of metal, used for boiling water	
key	1. used for locking and un-locking doors 2. a thing on a piano or type-writer which is pressed down by the fingers	**keyhole** **keyboard**
kick	to hit with the foot	**kicked** **kicking**
kidnap	to steal a person, usually a child	**kidnapped** **kidnapper** **kidnapping**
kill	to take life	**killed** **killer** **killing**
kilogramme	a measure of mass (weight) in the metric system	
kilometre	a measure of length in the metric system	
kilt	a short skirt with a pattern of crossing stripes	
kind	1. a sort 2. friendly: helpful	**kinder** **kindest** **kindhearted** **kindly** **kindness**
king	the head man of a country	
kingdom	a country with a king or queen	
kipper	a herring dried over smoke	

kiss	1. a touch with the lips as a sign of love	**kisses** **kissed**
	2. to give a kiss	**kisses** **kissing**
kitchen	the room where food is prepared	
kite	a light frame covered with paper or cloth that flies in the air at the end of a string	
kitten	a young cat	
knee	the joint in the middle of the leg	
kneel	to go down on one or both knees	**kneeled** **kneeler** **kneeling** **knelt**
knew	(Jill *knew* the answer to the question)	
knife	a blade on a handle, used for cutting	**knives**
knight	one of the king's noblemen	
knit	to weave with needles	**knitted** **knitter** **knitting**
knob	a rounded door handle	**knobbly**
knock	1. to make a sharp tap	**knocked**
	2. to hit	**knocker** **knocking**
knot	1. where string or rope is tied	**knotted**
	2. to make a knot	**knotting**
	3. a speed: one sea mile per hour	
know	1. to understand	**knew**
	2. to recognise	**knowing** **knowledge** **known**
knuckle	a joint in the fingers	

l

label	1. a slip of paper on some-thing to say what it is or where it is going 2. to put a label on	**labelled** **labelling**
laboratory	a place where scientific experiments are done	**laboratories**
labour	work	**labourer**
lace	1. a fancy net material made from woven thread 2. a piece of cord for tying 3. to tie up with a lace	**laced** **lacing** **shoelace**
lad	a boy	
ladder	a set of steps which can be moved	
ladle	a large spoon with a long handle	
lady	1. a woman 2. the wife of a nobleman	**ladies**
lady-bird	a small beetle that flies	
lag	to go slowly and not to keep up	**lagged** **lagging**
lagoon	a shallow lake of sea water	
laid	(The hen *laid* an egg)	
lair	place where a wild animal lives or hides	
lake	a stretch of water inland	
lamb	a young sheep	
lame	crippled: not able to walk properly	**lamely**
lamp	a light, usually covered by glass	**lamp-post**
land	1. the ground 2. to come on land or shore from an aeroplane or ship	**landed** **landing** **landslide**
landing	the flat space at the top of the stairs	

landlady	a lady who keeps a boarding house or inn, or who owns a house that is rented	**landladies**
landlord	a man who keeps an inn or boarding house, or who owns a house that is rented	
lane	a narrow road or pathway	
language	words used by people of a country	
lanky	tall and thin	
lantern	a case with glass sides, into which a light is put	
lap	1. the top part of the legs of someone sitting down	
	2. once round a race track	**lapped**
	3. to drink like a cat	**lapping**
larch	a large tree with cones	**larches**
lard	fat from pigs, used for cooking	
larder	a cool room or cupboard for storing food	
large	big: great	**enlarge**
		largely
		larger
		largest
lark	a bird that sings sweetly and flies very high	
lash	1. a hair on the eye-lid	**lashes**
	2. to bind tightly, usually with a rope	**lashed**
		lashes
	3. to whip fiercely	**lashing**
lass	a girl	**lasses**
lasso	a long rope with a loop at the end used by cowboys	**lassoes**
last	1. the shape of a foot, used by cobblers	
	2. after all the rest: at the end	**lasted**
	3. to keep going on	**lasting**
latch	a catch on a door or gate	**latches**
late	behind time	**lately**
		later
		latest

la le

lather	froth made when soap and water are well mixed	**lathered** **lathering**
laugh	1. a sound made when you are happy or amused 2. to show you are amused	**laughed** **laughing** **laughter**
launch	1. a small boat 2. to slide a boat into water	**launches** **launched** **launches** **launching**
laundry	a building where clothes are washed, dried and ironed	**laundries**
lava	molten rocks from a volcano	
lavatory	a toilet	**lavatories**
lavender	a plant that is very sweet-smelling	
law	a rule which must be obeyed	**lawful** **lawless** **unlawful**
lawn	ground covered with short grass in a garden or park	**lawn-mower**
lawyer	someone who knows a great deal about laws	
lay	1. to produce an egg 2. to set 3. (Yesterday I *lay* in the sun all day)	**laid** **laying**
lazy	idle: not wanting to work	**lazier** **laziest** **laziness**
lead	1. a heavy grey metal 2. a piece of thin leather used as a rein for a dog 3. to show the way 4. to be in first place	**leader** **leading** **led**
leaf	1. the green, flat part of a plant or tree 2. a sheet of paper in a book	**leaves** **leaflet** **leafy**
league	1. a group of teams that play each other 2. an old measure of distance	

leak	1. a crack or hole through which liquid can run in or out	**leaked** **leaking** **leaky**
	2. to let water in or out	
lean	1. thin	**leaned**
	2. without fat	**leaning**
	3. to slope	**leant**
leap	to jump	**leaped** **leaping** **leapt**
learn	to get to know something	**learned** **learner** **learning** **learnt**
least	the smallest	
leather	the skin of some animals prepared for use	**leathery**
leave	1. to go away from	**leaving**
	2. to allow to stay	**left**
led	(Our team *led* all the way)	
ledge	a narrow shelf	
leek	a vegetable like a long onion	
left	1. gone away	
	2. the opposite side to the right	
legend	an ancient story	
lemon	a sour yellow fruit	**lemonade**
lend	to let someone use something belonging to you	**lending** **lent**
length	how long something is from one end to the other	
lengthen	to make longer	**lengthened** **lengthening**
lens	a circular piece of glass for bending light	**lenses**
Lent	the six weeks before Easter	
lent	(John *lent* me his book so that I could read it)	
leopard	a fierce animal with spotted fur	

le li

less	not as much, or as many, as	
lesson	1. something you learn 2. the time spent in school on one subject at a time	
let	to allow	**letting**
letter	1. a written message sent to someone 2. the written shape of a sound; a part of the alphabet	
lettuce	a green-leaved plant used in salads	
level	1. flat or even 2. to flatten or to even up	**level- crossing levelled levelling**
lever	a rod or bar for lifting or moving things	
liar	someone who does not tell the truth	
library	1. a large number of books 2. a place where books are kept	**libraries**
licence	a form which gives you permission to do something	
lick	to touch with your tongue	**licked licking**
lie	1. an untruth 2. to say things which are untrue 3. to rest on your back or side	**lay lied lying**
life	1. the time from when you are born till when you die 2. being alive	**lives lifeless lifelike lifetime**
lift	1. a machine that takes you from floor to floor to save you using the stairs 2. to raise up	**lifted lifting**
lift-off	the moment when a space ship leaves the ground	

light	1. brightness 2. of little mass (weight) 3. to set on fire	**lighten** **lighter** **lightest** **lighting** **lightly** **lit**
lighthouse	a tower with a warning light for ships to see	
lightning	flashes of light in a thunderstorm	
like	1. the same or nearly the same as 2. to be fond of	**liked** **likely** **likeness**
lilac	1. a bush with white or mauve flowers 2. a mauve colour	
lily	a large flower with a long stem	
limb	an arm or a leg	
limit	boundary: the edge: the furthest you are allowed to go	
limp	1. the uneven walk of a lame person 2. drooping 3. to walk unevenly	**limped** **limping**
limpet	a shell-fish that sticks firmly to rocks	
line	1. a long, thin mark 2. a row 3. to cover the inside of a thing	**lined** **lining**
line up	to form a row	
linen	cloth made from flax	
liner	a large ship for carrying people	
link	1. one part of a chain 2. to join two things together	**linked** **linking**
linoleum	a material for covering floors	
lint	a soft cloth for putting on cuts	
lion	a large, fierce wild animal	**lioness**

liquid	anything that flows like water	
liquorice	a root used for making sweets	
lisp	to sound 's' and 'z' like 'th'	**lisped** **lisping**
list	a number of things written one under the other	
listen	to hear carefully	**listened** **listener** **listening**
lit	(Mother *lit* the fire to make us warm)	
litre	a measure of capacity in the metric system	
litter	1. rubbish or waste paper left lying about 2. a number of animals born at the same time 3. a kind of stretcher	
little	small	
live	to be alive	**lived** **living**
lively	full of life	**livelier** **liveliest**
lizard	a small reptile with short legs and a tail	
load	1. something to be carried 2. to put things on to something to be carried	**loaded** **loading**
loaf	bread baked in a shape	**loaves**
loan	1. something that is lent 2. to lend	**loaned** **loaning**
lobster	a shell-fish which has two big claws	
local	to do with a place or district	
loch	Scottish word for lake	
lock	1. a fastening which is opened or closed with a key 2. to fasten by turning the key in a lock	**locked** **locker** **locking**
locomotive	a railway engine	

lodge	1. a small house at the gates of a large house or castle 2. to live with for a time	lodged lodger lodging
loft	a store-room in a roof	lofty
lollipop	a sweet on a stick	
lonely	1. without friends 2. with no-one near	lonelier loneliest loneliness
long	of some length	longer longest
long for	to want something very much	longed longing
look	1. to turn one's eyes towards 2. to seem to be	looked looking
look for	to seek	
loom	1. a frame on which wool or cotton thread is woven 2. to appear gradually, as in a fog	loomed looming
loop	1. a ring made with wire, string or thread 2. to form a loop	looped looping
loose	1. free to move 2. to set free	loosely loosen loosened loosening looser loosest
lord	a nobleman	lordship
lorry	a motor truck for carrying loads	lorries
lose	1. to be unable to find something 2. to be beaten in a game	loser losing lost
loss	anything you lose	losses
loud	making a lot of noise	louder loudest loudly loud- speaker

lounge	a sitting-room	
love	1. goodness	**lovable**
	2. to be fond of	**loved**
		loving
		lovingly
lovely	beautiful: very pleasing	**lovelier**
		loveliest
		loveliness
low	not high or tall	**lower**
		lowest
luck	1. chance	**luckier**
	2. good fortune	**luckiest**
		luckily
		lucky
luggage	a traveller's baggage	
lukewarm	1. slightly warm	
	2. half-hearted	
lullaby	a song to help a baby go to sleep	**lullabies**
lumberjack	a person who cuts down trees for a living	
lump	1. a shapeless piece of anything	
	2. a swelling	
lunar	to do with the moon	
lunar module	the part of a space ship used for landing on the moon	
lunatic	a mad person	
lunch	a meal eaten in the middle of the day	**lunches**
lungs	the part of the body inside the chest where you breathe air	
lurk	to hide, in order to lie in wait	**lurked**
		lurking
luxury	something pleasant but not necessary	**luxuries**
lying	1. not telling the truth	
	2. (Daisy was *lying* on her bed)	
lynx	a kind of wild cat	**lynxes**

m

macaroni	tubes made from a wheat paste which become soft when they are cooked	
machine	something constructed, with moving parts, which helps to do work	
mackerel	a sea fish whose oily flesh is good to eat	**mackerel**
mackintosh	a raincoat	**mackin-toshes**
made	(Mary's mother *made* her a new dress)	
magazine	a book or paper that comes out regularly	
magic	1. when impossible things seem to come true 2. conjuring tricks	**magical**
magician	a person who does things which seem impossible	
magnet	a bar of iron to which some other metals will cling	**magnetised magnetising**
magnificent	splendid: grand to look at	
magnify	1. to make something seem bigger than it is by using a magnifying glass 2. to exaggerate	**magnified magnifies magnifying**
magpie	a black and white bird with a long tail	
maid	1. a young girl 2. a woman servant	
mail	anything sent by post	
main	most important	**mainly**
majesty	a title for a king or queen	**majesties**
make	1. to build or fit together 2. to force	**made maker making**

make up	to invent
male	a man or a boy
mammal	an animal, such as a dog or human, which has warm blood and feeds its young at the breast
manage	1. to be in charge of something 2. just to be able to do something

managed
manager
managing

mane	the long hair on the neck of a horse or lion
mangle	1. a machine which presses the water out of washing 2. to use a mangle

mangled
mangling

manner	1. the way someone behaves 2. the way a thing is done

mannered

mantelpiece	a shelf over the fireplace
manufacture	to make things in a factory
many	a lot: a big number
maple	a tree with broad leaves
marble	1. a hard stone which is usually beautifully marked 2. a small ball made of glass or clay, used for playing the game of 'marbles'
march	to walk like a soldier

marched
marches
marching

March	the third month of the year
mare	a female horse
margarine	a food that can be used instead of butter
margin	a blank space at the sides of a page
marigold	an orange-coloured flower
mark	1. a sign or a stain 2. to put a mark on something 3. to correct someone's work

marked
marker
marking

market	a place, often in the open, for buying and selling things	
marmalade	jam made with oranges	
maroon	1. a dark red colour 2. to leave someone alone on a desert island	**marooned** **marooning**
marriage	when two people get married	
marrow	a long-shaped green vegetable	
marry	to take a husband or wife	**married** **marries** **marrying**
marsh	a piece of boggy ground	**marshes** **marshy**
marvellous	wonderful	**marvellously**
mash	to press into small pieces and mix up	**mashed** **mashes** **mashing**
mask	a cover worn over the face so that the person cannot be recognised	**masked**
mass	1. a large amount of something 2. weight 3. a church service	**masses** **massive**
mast	a tall pole for the sails of a ship or for a flag	
master	a man in charge	
match	1. a piece of wood with a special tip which lights if it is rubbed 2. a game between two sides 3. to be alike in colour or shape	**matches** **matched** **matches** **matching**
mate	1. a partner 2. a friend 3. the person next in command to the captain of a ship	
material	the stuff of which a thing is made	

mathematics	the study of numbers and measurement	**mathe-matical**
matter	to be important	
mattress	the soft part of the bed on which you lie	**mattresses**
mauve	a light purple colour	
maximum	the greatest amount	
May	the fifth month of the year	
mayor	the chief person in a town	**mayoress**
maypole	a pole, with ribbons, for dancing round	
meadow	grassland	
meal	the food you eat at one time	
mean	1. selfish 2. to intend to do something	**meaning** **meant**
measles	an illness which shows by red spots on your body	
measure	to find out the size of something	**measured** **measure-ment** **measuring**
meat	the animal flesh we eat	
mechanic	someone who works with machines	**mechanical**
medal	a small piece of decorated metal given to brave people or to the winners of a game or sport	
meddle	to interfere with something that should be left alone	**meddled** **meddling**
medicine	a liquid or pill which you swallow when you are ill	
meet	1. to come together 2. to touch or join	**meeting** **met**
melon	a very large fruit	
melt	to make solid things into liquid by heating	**melted** **melting**
member	someone who belongs to a group	

memory	1. the power of remembering	
	2. something you can remember	**memorise**
mend	to repair	**mended**
		mender
		mending
mental	of the mind: worked out in your head and not on paper	
menu	a list of what there is to eat	
mercy	pity: forgiveness	**merciful**
mermaid	a sea-woman found in stories, with the tail of a fish	
merry	happy: full of fun	**merrier**
		merriest
		merrily
mess	a dirty or untidy muddle	**messy**
message	news sent from one person to another	
messenger	someone who carries a message	
metal	a material such as iron or steel or gold	
meteor	a shooting star	**meteorite**
meter	a machine for measuring	
method	a way of doing something	**methodical**
metre	measure of length in the metric system	**metric**
mice	more than one mouse	
microbe	a minute germ	
microphone	the instrument into which you speak when broadcasting	
microscope	an instrument for making tiny objects appear much larger	
midday	noon	
middle	the centre	
midnight	12 o'clock at night	
midsummer	half-way through the summer	

mi

might	1. great power or strength	**mighty**
	2. (I *might* go for a walk if the weather were fine)	
mile	a measure of distance	**mileage**
		milestone
milk	1. white liquid which we get mostly from cows	**milked**
		milking
	2. to get milk from an animal	**milkman**
mill	1. a place where corn is ground	**miller**
	2. a factory	
millilitre	measure of capacity in the metric system	
millimetre	measure of length in the metric system	
million	1 000 000	
millionaire	a person who is very rich	
mince	to cut into very small pieces	**minced**
		mincer
		mincing
mincemeat	a mixture of chopped dried fruits used in mince pies	
mind	1. the part of the brain with which you think	
	2. to be careful	**minded**
	3. to keep safe	**minder**
		minding
mine	1. a deep hole or tunnel in the ground from which coal and other minerals are dug	**mined**
		miner
		mining
	2. a sort of bomb placed under the ground or under water	
	3. belonging to me	
mineral	a material, such as coal or metal, that is dug from the ground	
mint	1. a plant used for making some foods tasty	
	2. the place where coins are made	

minus	take away (ten *minus* four leaves six)	
minute	1. 60 seconds 2. very small	
miracle	a wonderful happening that cannot be explained	**miraculous**
mirror	a looking glass	
misbehave	to behave badly	**misbehaved** **misbehaving** **misbehaviour**
mischief	something which causes people annoyance or harm	**mischievous**
miser	a very mean person who tries not to spend his money	**miserly**
miserable	unhappy	**miserably** **misery**
misfortune	bad luck	
miss	1. the title sometimes given to a girl or lady who is not married	**misses**
	2. to feel the loss of	**missed**
	3. not to hit	**misses** **missing**
mist	cloud at ground level	**misty**
mistake	1. something that has been done wrongly 2. to believe wrongly	**mistaken** **mistaking** **mistook**
mistletoe	a plant with white berries which we hang up at Christmas time	
mistress	1. a woman who teaches 2. a woman who looks after a house	**mistresses**
mitten	a glove which does not cover the ends of the fingers	
mix	to stir together	**mixed** **mixer** **mixes** **mixing** **mixture**

moan	1. a long, low sound made when you are very sad or in pain 2. to make such a sound	**moaned** **moaning**
moat	a large ditch round a castle	
mock	to make fun of	**mocked** **mocking**
model	1. a small copy of something 2. a good example 3. to shape	**modelled** **modelling**
modern	up-to-date	
moist	slightly wet	**moisten** **moisture**
mole	a small animal, with a pointed nose, that lives underground	
molten	melted	
moment	a very small space of time	
monastery	a building where monks live	**monasteries**
Monday	the second day of the week	
money	coins or banknotes	
mongrel	a dog of no special kind	
monitor	someone who does jobs for a teacher	
monk	a holy man who usually lives in a monastery	
monkey	a little animal that lives in trees in hot countries	
monster	a large, frightening creature	**monstrous**
month	one of the twelve parts of a year	**monthly**
moon	a planet that moves round the earth	**moonbeam** **moonlight** **moonlit**
moor	1. open heathland 2. to tie up a boat or ship	**moored** **mooring**
moose	a large deer	
mop	1. a bundle of cloth on the end of a stick for cleaning floors 2. to wipe with a mop	**mopped** **mopping**

more	greater than	
morning	before midday	
mosquito	a tiny insect that flies and bites	**mosquitoes**
moss	a short thick-growing plant found in shady or damp places	**mossy**
most	greatest or largest	**mostly**
moth	an insect like a butterfly which usually flies by night	
mother	a woman who has children	
motor	a machine that makes something move	**motor-boat** **motor-car** **motor-cycle** **motorist** **motorway**
mould	1. a hairy growth caused by damp 2. a shape in which things are pressed or put to set 3. to shape something by using a mould	**moulded** **moulding** **mouldy**
mount	1. to get on to a horse 2. to climb	**mounted** **mounting**
mountain	a high hill	**mountainous**
mouse	a small rat-like animal	**mice**
moustache	the hair on a man's top lip	
mouth	1. the opening through which we eat and speak 2. where a river meets the sea 3. the entrance to anything	
move	1. to put in another place 2. to go to live in another place	**movable** **moved** **movement** **moving**
mow	to cut grass with a machine	**mowed** **mower** **mowing** **mown**
much	a great deal	
muddle	1. untidiness: a jumble 2. to make a muddle	**muddled** **muddling**

mu my

muddy	thick with mud	**muddier** **muddiest**
multiply	to add together an amount a number of times	**multiplica- tion** **multiplied** **multiplies** **multiplying**
mumble	to speak without opening your mouth properly	**mumbled** **mumbling**
mummy	1. a child's word for mother 2. a dead body which has been saved from decay	**mummies**
mumps	an illness which causes swellings of the face and neck	
murder	to kill someone	**murdered** **murderer** **murdering** **murderous**
muscle	(The boxer showed us the strong *muscle* in his arm)	
museum	a building where interesting things are put on show	
mushroom	a white and brown plant shaped like a tiny umbrella	
music	a pleasing sound played or sung	**musical**
musician	someone who plays music	
must	(You *must* do what you are told)	
mustard	a plant whose seed is used to make the hot yellow mixture sometimes eaten with meat	
mutton	meat we get from sheep	
myself	(I am sitting by *myself* as my partner is away)	
mystery	something that cannot be explained	**mysteries** **mysterious** **mysteriously**

n

nag	1. a horse 2. to be always finding fault with	**nagged** **nagging**
nail	1. a piece of metal driven into wood to hold it in place 2. the horny part at the end of the fingers and toes	**nailed** **nailing**
naked	bare	
name	1. a word by which someone or something is known 2. to call something or someone by a name	**named** **naming**
narrow	not wide	**narrower** **narrowest** **narrowly**
nasty	not pleasant	**nastier** **nastiest** **nastily**
nation	a country and its people	**national**
native	a native of a country is a person who was born in that country	
natural	1. not artificial 2. at ease	**naturally**
nature	everything in the world not made by people	
naughty	badly behaved	**naughtier** **naughtiest** **naughtily**
navigate	to guide the course of a ship or aircraft	**navigated** **navigating** **navigation**
navy	warships and their crews	**navies**
near	not far off	**nearby** **nearer** **nearest** **nearly**

neat	tidy: trim	**neater** **neatest** **neatly** **neatness**
necessary	cannot be done without	**necessity**
neck	the part of the body which joins the head and shoulders	
necklace	a thread of beads or jewels worn round the neck	
need	1. a want 2. to want	**needed** **needing** **needy**
needle	1. used for sewing with cotton or wool 2. a pointer on a dial	**needlework**
neglect	not to bother about	**neglected** **neglecting**
neigh	1. the sound a horse makes 2. to make a sound like a horse	**neighed** **neighing**
neighbour	a person who lives next door or nearby	**neighbour-** **hood**
neither	not one or the other	
nephew	the son of a brother or sister	
nerve	1. one of the parts of the body which carries messages to and from the brain 2. bravery: cheek	
nervous	easily frightened	**nervously**
nest	a home which birds make	**nested** **nesting**
netball	a ball game	
nettle	a stinging weed	
never	at no time	
new	fresh	**newer** **newest** **newly**
newsagent	a person who sells newspapers in a shop	

newspaper	a paper that gives news	
newsreel	a news film	
newt	a creature like a small lizard which lives in and out of water	
next	1. the one after 2. closest to	
nibble	to eat in small bites	**nibbled** **nibbling**
nice	pretty: pleasing	**nicely** **nicer** **nicest**
nickname	a name given in fun	
niece	the daughter of your brother or sister	
night	the time when it is dark	**nightdress** **nightgown** **nightly** **night-time**
nightingale	a bird with a lovely song	
nightmare	a frightening dream	
nine	9	**ninth**
nineteen	19	**nineteenth**
ninety	90	**ninetieth**
nobleman	a lord	**noblemen**
nobody	no one	
nod	to move your head up and down	**nodded** **nodding**
noise	a loud sound, usually unpleasant	**noisier** **noisiest** **noisily** **noisy**
none	not one	
nonsense	something silly	
noon	midday	
normal	usual	**normally**
north	opposite to south	
nose	part of the face with which you smell	
notch	a small 'v' shaped cut	**notches**

note	1. a short piece of writing	**notebook**
	2. a musical sound	**noted**
	3. to look and remember	**notepaper**
		noting
nothing	not anything at all	
notice	1. a printed warning or guide	**noticed**
	2. to see	**noticing**
nought	nothing	
November	the eleventh month of the year	
nowhere	in no place	
nozzle	a spout at the end of a pipe	
nucleus	the centre around which things are grouped	**nuclei** **nuclear**
nuisance	someone or something that annoys you	
numb	not able to feel anything	**numbed**
number	how many	**numbered**
numerator	the number above the line in a fraction	
nurse	1. one who looks after children or sick people	**nursed** **nursery**
	2. to look after someone who cannot look after herself	**nursing**
	3. to hold a child in your arms	
nylon	a hard-wearing artificial thread	

O

oak	1. a tree on which acorns grow	
	2. wood from the oak tree	
oar	a wooden pole with a wide flat end, used for rowing a boat	
oasis	a place in the desert where there is water, and things grow	**oases**

oath	1. a promise 2. a curse	
oats	a kind of corn used for food	
obedient	doing as you are told	**obedience** **obediently**
obey	to do as you are told	**obeyed** **obeying**
object	1. any article 2. an aim 3. to announce that you dis- like something or someone	**objected** **objecting** **objection**
oblige	to do someone a favour	**obliged** **obliging**
oblong	a four-sided figure which is longer than it is broad	
oboe	a musical wind instrument	
obstacle	something that is in the way	
obstinate	stubborn	
obtain	to get	**obtained** **obtaining**
obvious	easy to see or understand	**obviously**
occupy	1. to live in 2. to take possession of a country	**occupation** **occupied** **occupies** **occupying**
ocean	a large sea	
o'clock	of the clock	
October	the tenth month of the year	
octopus	a sea animal with eight arms	**octopuses**
odd	1. queer 2. uneven 3. not one of a pair	**oddly**
off	1. not on 2. away	
offend	1. to hurt the feelings of 2. to do wrong	**offended** **offending**
offer	to say or show that you are ready to give or do anything that is needed	**offered** **offering**

office	a place where business is carried on
officer	a person in charge
often	many times
oil	1. a greasy liquid which keeps machinery running smoothly **oiled** **oiling** 2. to put oil on something **oily**
ointment	a grease that you put on a cut
old	having lasted for a long time **olden** **older** **oldest** **old-fashioned**
once	at one time only
one	a single thing: 1
onion	a white bulb with a strong smell, used as a vegetable
only	by itself
open	not shut or covered **opened** **opener** **opening** **openly**
operate	1. to work **operated** 2. to cut open the body of a **operating** sick person **operation** **operator**
opinion	what you think is true
opponent	a person who is against you
opposite	1. something that is quite different from something else 2. face to face with
orange	1. a fruit 2. the colour of an orange
orangeade	a drink made from orange juice
orbit	the path in which one thing moves round another in space
orchard	a field full of fruit trees

orchestra	a group of people playing musical instruments	
order	1. a command 2. a tidy arrangement 3. a list of things you want from a shop 4. to tell someone to do something	**ordered** **ordering**
ordinary	usual: not surprising	
organ	a musical instrument worked by air and often used in churches	**organist**
ornament	1. a decoration which makes something more beautiful 2. a vase or piece of pottery in a room	
orphan	a child whose father and mother are dead	**orphanage** **orphaned**
ostrich	a very large bird which cannot fly	ostriches
other	1. different 2. more	**otherwise**
otter	an animal which lives in water	
ought	(You *ought* to help your parents when they are busy)	
ounce	a measure of mass (weight): 16 ounces make 1 pound	
our	belonging to us	
ourselves out	us or we 1. not in 2. not burning	**outdoors** **outer**
outing	a pleasure trip	
outlaw	a bandit: a person who does not keep the law	
outside	1. the outer part: the covering 2. not indoors	
oval	egg-shaped	
oven	a closed space in which we cook food	

over	1. above 2. across 3. finished	
overalls	clothes to put on over your suit or dress to keep it clean	
overboard	over the side of a ship	
overcoat	a top coat	
overhead	above your head: up in the sky	
overseas	in a land across the sea	
overtake	to catch up with and pass	**overtaken** **overtaking** **overtook**
overtime	extra time spent by a person at a job	
overturn	to turn upside-down	**overturned** **overturning**
owe	not to have paid for something which you have had	**owed** **owing**
owl	a bird of prey which hoots and flies at night	
own	1. to have something which belongs to you 2. to admit 3. (I like to have my *own* way)	**owned** **owner** **owning**
ox	an animal like a cow	**oxen**
oxygen	one of the gases in the air	
oyster	a shell-fish	

p

pace	a stride or step	
pack	1. a set of playing cards 2. a bundle, usually carried on on the back 3. to put into boxes, bags or cases	**packed** **packet** **packing** **unpack**

pad	1. a cover to protect your leg while playing cricket 2. to stuff with soft material	**padded** **padding**
paddle	1. a short oar 2. to use a paddle 3. to walk in shallow water with bare feet	**paddled** **paddling**
page	1. one side of a leaf in a book 2. a boy attendant	
paid	(John *paid* for his school dinners and then lost the change)	
pail	a bucket	
pain	suffering: an ache	**pained** **painful** **painfully** **paining** **painless**
paint	1. a liquid for colouring things 2. to put paint on to something	**paintbox** **painted** **painter** **painting**
pair	a set of two: two things that are alike or go together	
palace	a special house for a king or queen or bishop	
pale	faint in colour	**paleness**
palm	1. a tree that grows in hot countries 2. part of your hand	
pancake	a thin flat batter cake	
pane	a sheet of glass in a window	
panic	sudden fear and alarm	
pansy	a flower like a large violet	**pansies**
pant	to gasp in quick breaths	**panted** **panting**
panther	a kind of leopard	
pantomime	a play based on a fairy story, usually performed at Christmas time	

pantry	a room or large cupboard for storing food	**pantries**
paper	the stuff on which we write, draw or paint	
papyrus	an ancient kind of paper	
parachute	nylon cloth which opens in the shape of an umbrella to save a person who has to jump from an aircraft	**parachutist** **paratroops**
paragraph	a short part of a piece of writing	
paraffin	a thin oil used in heaters	
parallel	the same distance apart all along	**parallelo- gram**
parcel	something wrapped up in paper and tied with string	
pardon	1. forgiveness 2. to forgive or excuse some- one	**pardoned** **pardoning**
parent	a father or mother	
park	1. a piece of ground where people go to enjoy them- selves 2. to put a car in a place and leave it there	**car-park** **parked** **parking**
parliament	the people chosen by election who decide a country's laws	
parrot	a bird with bright feathers, often kept as a pet	
parsley	a plant used for flavouring food	
parsnip	a plant whose thick root is used as food	
part	1. a piece of something: a share 2. to separate	**parted** **parting** **partition** **partly**
particle	a very small piece	

partner	someone who shares work or play with another person	
party	a number of people having a jolly time together	parties
pass	1. a narrow path through the mountains 2. a ticket 3. to go by 4. to hand on 5. to get through an examination	passes **passed** **passes** **passing** **passport**
passage	1. a corridor 2. a voyage from one port to another	
passenger	a traveller on a train, bus, car, ship or aircraft	
past	(We start school at half *past* one)	
paste	1. sticky stuff which is put on to things to fix them together 2. to stick with paste	**pasted** **pasting**
pastry	1. the crust of pies or tarts 2. a pie, tart or cake	pastries
pasture	a field in which cattle feed	
patch	1. a piece of material sewn over a hole to mend it 2. to put a patch on something	patches **patched** **patches** **patching** **patchy**
path	a place for walking: a track	**pathway**
patience	1. calmness when you are annoyed, or in trouble, or waiting 2. a card game	**patiently**
patient	1. a person having treatment from a doctor 2. having patience	
pattern	1. something to be copied 2. a design	

pavement	a footpath of flat stones beside a road	
paw	an animal's foot with claws	
pay	to give money for something	**paid** **paying** **payment**
pea	a green seed which grows in a pod and which is eaten as a vegetable	
peace	1. quietness and calm 2. a time when there is no war	**peaceful** **peacefully**
peach	a fruit with a skin like velvet	**peaches**
peacock	a bird with a large tail which can open like a fan	
peak	1. the top of a mountain 2. the front of a cap	**peaked**
peal	the sound of bells or thunder	
pear	a juicy fruit with yellow or green skin	
pearl	a whitish jewel which is found inside the shell of a pearl oyster	**pearly**
pebble	a small round stone	**pebbly**
peck	to bite or pick up food with a beak	**pecked** **pecking**
peculiar	odd: unusual	
pedal	1. part of a machine, worked by the foot 2. to use a pedal	**pedalled** **pedalling**
pedestrian	a person who is walking	
peel	1. the outer skin of a fruit or vegetable 2. to take off the outer skin of something	**peeled** **peeler** **peeling**
peep	to look at something quickly while you are hidden	**peeped** **peeping**
pelt	1. the skin and fur of an animal 2. to throw things at somebody or something	**pelted** **pelting**

penalty	punishment for breaking the law: a free kick at goal given against a team that has broken a rule	**penalties**
pence	pennies	
pencil	1. a pointed writing tool with a black or coloured centre 2. to use a pencil	**pencil-box** **pencilled** **pencilling**
pendulum	a hanging mass (weight) that swings freely	
penknife	a small pocket knife	**penknives**
penny	a coin: one hundred make one pound	**pennies**
penguin	a sea bird of the southern part of the world that can swim but not fly	
people	human beings	
pepper	(We put *pepper* and salt on our dinner)	
perch	1. anything on which a bird stands 2. to settle on a perch	**perches** **perched** **perches** **perching**
percussion	musical instruments which are struck to be played	
perfect	exactly right	**perfectly**
perform	1. to do something 2. to sing, act or dance in public	**perform-ance** **performed** **performer** **performing**
perfume	scent	
perhaps	possibly	
perimeter	the distance round the edge of something	
permission	(The teacher gave Tina *permission* to leave the room)	
permit	to allow	**permitted** **permitting**
perpendicular	exactly upright	

pe ph pi

person	a human being	
perspire	to sweat	**perspiration** **perspired** **perspiring**
persuade	to talk to someone to get them to do what you want	**persuaded** **persuading**
pest	a person or thing which is a nuisance	
petal	a part of a flower	
petrol	the fuel used by motor cars	
phone	the telephone	
photograph	a picture taken by a camera	**photo-grapher** **photo-graphy**
pianist	someone who plays a piano	
piano	a musical instrument played by pressing down keys	
pick	1. a pointed hammer for breaking hard ground 2. to choose 3. to gather fruit, flowers or vegetables	**picked** **picking**
pickle	vegetables kept in vinegar	
picnic	1. a meal eaten out in the country 2. to have a picnic	**picnicked** **picnicker** **picnicking**
picture	a drawing, painting or photograph	
piece	part of something	
pier	a long platform built out into the sea	
pigeon	a bird of the dove family	
pigmy	one of a race of very small people living in parts of Africa and Asia	**pigmies**
pigtail	a plait of hair	
pile	1. a heap 2. to make a heap	**piled** **piling**

pilgrim	a person who makes a journey to a holy place	**pilgrimage**
pill	medicine taken as a tablet	
pillar	a tall post made of stone to support part of a large building	
pillow	a cushion on which to rest your head in bed	**pillowcase**
pilot	a person who steers a plane or boat	
pimple	a sore little swelling on the skin	
pinafore	an apron or overall	
pincers	a tool for pulling out nails	
pinch	to squeeze sharply	**pinched** **pinches** **pinching**
pine	a tree on which cones grow and which has leaves like needles	
pineapple	a large fruit shaped like a pine cone	
pink	pale red	
pint	eight of them make a gallon	
pioneer	someone who does or tries something first	
pipe	1. a tube 2. something in which to smoke tobacco	**piping**
pirate	a sea-robber who steals from ships at sea	
pistol	a small gun	
piston	part of an engine which moves up and down in a cylinder	
pitch	1. a piece of ground on which a game is played 2. black tarry stuff used in making roads 3. to throw	**pitches** **pitched** **pitches** **pitching**

pity — a feeling of sorrow for a person who has had trouble or bad luck

place
1. a spot or position — **placed**
2. to put something in position — **placing**

plaice — a flat fish which is good to eat — **plaice**

plain
1. a stretch of level country — **plainly**
2. not pretty
3. easy to see or understand
4. simple

plait — a rope of hair made by twisting three lengths of it together — **plaited**

plan
1. a drawing to show how a thing looks from above — **planned**
2. something you intend to do — **planner**
3. to arrange to do something — **planning**

plane — an aeroplane

plane
1. a tool for smoothing wood — **planed**
2. a tree like a sycamore — **planing**
3. to smooth wood with a plane

planet — a large object in space which, like the earth, moves round the sun

plank — a long flat piece of wood

plant
1. something that grows in the ground — **planted**
2. to put something in the ground so that it will grow — **planting**

plaster
1. a strip of cloth with a sticky side for covering cuts
2. a coating for walls and ceilings

plastic — a type of artificial material used for making toys, buckets, bowls and many other things

plasticine — a material used for modelling

plate — a flat dish on which food is put — **plateful**

platform	1. the raised part of a station on to which you step when getting off a train 2. the raised part of a floor, usually at one end of a hall	
play	1. a story told by acting 2. to join in a game	**played** **player** **playful** **playground** **playing** **playtime**
pleasant	cheerful: enjoyable	**pleasantly**
please	to give pleasure to someone	**pleased** **pleasing**
pleasure	enjoyment	
plenty	all that is needed and more	**plentiful**
pliers	a tool used for gripping things	
plimsoll	a light canvas shoe	
plod	to walk slowly and heavily	**plodded** **plodding**
plot	1. a small piece of land 2. a secret plan to do something 3. to make a plot	**plotted** **plotting**
plough	1. a machine used by farmers to turn over the soil 2. to use a plough	**ploughed** **ploughing**
pluck	1. courage 2. to pull out feathers 3. to pull a string or wire sharply	**plucked** **pluckily** **plucking** **plucky**
plug	1. something used to stop or fill up a hole 2. to put a plug in	**plugged** **plugging**
plum	a fruit with a stone in	
plumber	a person who fits and mends pipes for gas and water	
plump	fat: stout	
plunge	to move downwards very quickly	**plunged** **plunging**

plywood	strong board made by gluing layers of wood together	
poach	1. to steal animals or birds or fish from someone's land 2. to cook opened eggs or fish in boiling water	**poached** **poacher** **poaches** **poaching**
pocket	a little bag sewn into clothes	
poem	writing in verses where the lines usually rhyme with each other	
poet	a person who writes poems	
poetry	poems	
point	1. the sharp end of something 2. part of the score in a game 3. to show something with the finger	**pointed** **pointer** **pointing**
poison	1. something which, if eaten or drunk, will harm a living thing 2. to injure or kill a living thing with poison	**poisoned** **poisonous**
poke	to push the end of something into something else	**poked** **poking**
poker	a rod for poking a fire	
polar	to do with the North or South Pole	
pole	1. the parts of the earth which are furthest from the equator 2. a long round piece of wood	
police	people who help to keep law and order	**police**
polish	1. something used to make things shine 2. to rub something to make it shine	**polished** **polishes** **polishing**
polite	well-mannered	**politely** **politeness**
polythene	a strong plastic material	
pond	a small lake	
pony	a small horse	**ponies**

pool	a pond	
poor	1. having only a little money	**poorer**
	2. not well done	**poorest**
	3. not good	**poorly**
pop	short for popular	
poplar	a tall tree	
poppy	a plant with bright red flowers	**poppies**
popular	well-liked	
population	the number of people living in a place	
porch	the covered entrance to a building	**porches**
porcupine	an animal like a large hedge-hog	
pork	meat from a pig	
porpoise	a sea animal like a small whale	
porridge	cooked oats usually eaten for breakfast	
port	1. a town with a harbour or docks	
	2. the left-hand side of a ship or aeroplane	
	3. a wine	
portable	easy to carry	
porter	a person who carries luggage	
position	a place: a spot	
possess	to own something	**possessed**
		possesses
		possessing
		possession
		possessive
possible	1. able to be done	**impossible**
	2. able to happen	**possibility**
		possibly
post	1. a strong pole	**postbox**
	2. the carrying of letters and parcels	**postcard**
		posted
	3. the day's letters	**posting**
	4. to send letters or parcels by post	**postman**

po pr

poster	a large notice to advertise something	
potato	a vegetable which grows under the ground	**potatoes**
pottery	clay shaped into such things as cups, vases and plates and baked hard	
pouch	a small bag	**pouches**
pounce	to spring forward suddenly	**pounced** **pouncing**
pound	1. a measure of weight: 16 ounces 2. 100 pennies	
pour	1. to tip a liquid out of its container 2. to rain heavily	**poured** **pouring**
powder	1. dust made by crushing something 2. to crush something to powder	**powdered** **powdering** **powdery**
power	strength	**powerful** **powerless**
practically	almost	
practice	doing something many times	
practise	to do something many times in order to become better at it	**practised** **practising**
prairie	a wide area of flat grassland	
praise	to say something is good or well done	**praised** **praising**
pram	used for wheeling babies about	
pray	to speak to God, silently or aloud	**prayed** **prayer** **praying**
preach	to give a sermon	**preached** **preacher** **preaches** **preaching**
precious	valuable	
precipice	a steep cliff	

prefect   a pupil who makes other school-children keep the school rules

prefer   to like one thing or person better than another   **preferred** **preferring**

prepare   to get ready   **preparation** **prepared** **preparing**

present   1. a gift   **presented**
2. now   **presenting**
3. here: not away   **presently**
4. to give something

press   1. a machine for pressing, such as a printing machine   **presses** **pressed**
2. to squeeze or push something   **presses** **pressing**
3. to flatten or smooth with an iron

pretend   to make-believe   **pretended** **pretending**

pretty   pleasing to look at   **prettier** **prettiest** **prettily** **prettiness**

prevent   to stop something from happening   **prevented** **preventing** **prevention**

prey   an animal that is being hunted

price   the cost of something   **priceless**

prick   to make a small hole with a sharp point   **pricked** **pricking**

prickle   a thorn   **prickly**

pride   a feeling that you have done something well

priest   1. a Protestant or a Roman Catholic clergyman   **priestess**
2. a man appointed to organise worship in many religions

prime   a prime number is one that has no factors except itself and 1

primrose	a pale yellow spring flower	
prince	a boy of royal birth	
princess	a royal female	princesses
print	to make words or pictures with a printing machine	**printed** **printer** **printing**
prison	a place where criminals are kept	**prisoner**
private	not for everybody to know or use	**privately**
prize	a reward to be won	
probable	likely to happen	**probably**
problem	a puzzle: a question which needs to be carefully thought about	
proceed	to go on: to go forward	
procession	a group of people or things moving forward	
prod	to poke with something pointed like a stick	**prodded** **prodding**
produce	1. food that is grown 2. to make or show	**produced** **producing** **product** **production**
professor	an important teacher in a college or university	
profit	1. gain 2. to gain	**profited** **profiting**
programme	1. a plan 2. a list of items in a concert or play	
progress	1. improvement 2. to move forward: to get better	**progressed** **progresses** **progressing**
project	a plan of something to be done	
projector	a machine for showing films on a screen	
promenade	a paved road for walking on by the sea	

promise	to mean it when you say that you will do something	**promised** **promising**
prong	one of the points of a fork	**pronged**
proof	something that shows a thing is true	
propeller	blades which go round to move along an aircraft or ship	
proper	right: correct: suitable	**properly**
property	something owned by someone	properties
prosecute	to say in court that someone has done something against the law	**prosecuted** **prosecuting** **prosecution**
protect	to keep someone or something from harm or damage	**protected** **protecting** **protection**
protest	to object to something	**protested** **protesting**
proud	thinking highly of yourself	**proudly**
prove	to show that something is true	**proved** **proving**
proverb	a well-known saying which teaches a lesson	
provide	to supply	**provided** **providing**
prow	the front part of a boat	
prowl	to creep about, usually in search of something	**prowled** **prowler** **prowling**
prune	a dried plum	
public	1. all the people 2. for everyone to use	
pudding	a soft sweet food	
puddle	a little pool of water	
puff	1. a quick short blow of air or smoke 2. a soft pad for putting on face powder 3. to blow out steam or smoke in puffs	**puffed** **puffing**

pull	to tug towards yourself	**pulled**
		pulling
pulley	a wheel with a rope round it for lifting things	
pullover	a jersey or sweater	
pulse	the throbbing of blood through the body	
pump	1. a machine for forcing air or water through a tube	**pumped**
		pumping
	2. an indoor or dancing shoe	
	3. to use a pump	
punch	1. a blow with the fist	**punches**
	2. to use the fist for hitting	**punched**
		punches
		punching
punctual	on time	**punctuality**
puncture	1. a small hole made with a sharp point	**punctured**
		puncturing
	2. to make a hole	
punish	to make someone suffer for what he has done wrong	**punished**
		punishes
		punishing
		punishment
pupil	1. a person who is being taught	
	2. part of the eye	
puppet	a doll made to move, usually by strings	
puppy	a young dog	**puppies**
purchase	to buy	**purchased**
		purchasing
pure	clean: not mixed with anything else	
purple	the colour made when red and blue are mixed	
purpose	something that you mean to do	**purposely**
purr	1. the sound a cat makes when it is happy	**purred**
		purring
	2. to make a sound like a cat	

purse	a small bag for carrying money	
push	to press against something	**pushed** **pushes** **pushing**
put	to place in position	**putting**
putty	paste used for fixing glass in frames	
puzzle	1. a problem: something that is hard to work out 2. to think hard about a difficult question	**puzzled** **puzzling**
pyjamas	a suit to sleep in	
pylon	a tall tower, usually for carry-electric cables	
pyramid	a solid shape with triangular sides which meet at a point	
python	a large snake	

q

quack	1. the noise made by a duck 2. to make a noise like a duck	**quacked** **quacking**
quaint	odd: unusual: old-fashioned	
quantity	amount	**quantities**
quarrel	1. an angry disagreement 2. to argue: to disagree	**quarrelled** **quarrelling** **quarrelsome**
quarry	a place where stone is cut from the ground	**quarries**
quart	two pints	
quarter	one of four equal parts of anything	
quay	a place where ships load and unload	**quayside**
queen	1. the head woman of a country 2. the wife of a king	
queer	odd	**queerly**

quench   1. to cure a thirst   **quenched**
               2. to put out a fire   **quenches**
                                             quenching

question   1. something you say that   **questioned**
                  needs an answer   **questioning**
               2. to ask a question

queue   1. a line of people waiting   **queued**
                  their turn   **queueing**
               2. to form part of a queue

quick   speedy: lively   **quicker**
                                             quickest
                                             quickly
                                             quickness

quiet   1. making little or no noise   **quieter**
               2. still   **quietest**
                                             quietly

quill   a large feather

quilt   a padded bed cover   **quilted**

quite   completely

quiz   questions that test someone's **quizzes**
               knowledge

r

rabbit   a small, furry, long-eared
               animal that lives in a burrow

race   1. a kind of people   **raced**
               2. a test to see who is the   **racer**
                  fastest   **racing**

rack   a frame with bars or pegs for
               holding things

racket   1. a lot of noise
               2. a stringed bat used in
                  games like tennis (some-
                  times spelt racquet)

radar   a way of finding the position
               of aircraft or ships by elec-
               trical echoes

radiator	1. a number of hot-water pipes joined together and used for heating a room 2. the place in a motor-car, usually in the front, where hot water from the engine is cooled	
radio	a wireless set	
radish	a small vegetable eaten raw	radishes
radius	the distance from the centre of a circle to its edge	radii
raffia	narrow strips from palm-leaves, used for weaving into mats and baskets	
raft	floating logs or boards fastened together	
rafter	a beam of a roof	
rage	1. temper: great anger 2. to shout in great anger	**raged** **raging**
ragged	in torn clothes	
raid	1. a sudden attack 2. to attack suddenly	**raided** **raider** **raiding**
rail	a bar of wood or metal to hold on to or for a train to run on	**railing** **railway**
rain	1. drops of water falling from the clouds 2. to pour or shower down from above	**raincoat** **raindrop** **rained** **rainfall** **raining** **rainy**
rainbow	a coloured arch formed in the sky when the sun shines on falling rain	
raise	1. to lift up 2. to collect 3. to bring up	**raised** **raising**
raisin	a dried grape	

rake	1. a garden tool with a metal comb at the end 2. to use a rake	**raked** **raking**
ram	a male sheep	
ramble	1. a stroll 2. to roam or wander about	**rambled** **rambler** **rambling**
ramp	a short slope	
ranch	a large cattle farm	**ranches**
rang	(I *rang* the bell at playtime)	
rank	a person's title or position	
ransom	money paid to set someone free	
rare	uncommon: valuable	**rarely**
rascal	a rogue	
rash	1. a lot of red spots on the skin 2. thoughtless	**rashly**
rasher	a thin slice of bacon or ham	
raspberry	a small, sweet red fruit	**raspberries**
rate	1. speed 2. a set price	
rather	(I would *rather* drink milk than water)	
rattle	1. a baby's toy 2. a sharp clattering sound 3. to make a clattering sound	**rattled** **rattling**
raven	a large black bird	
ravine	a deep gorge	
raw	1. not cooked 2. very cold and damp	
ray	a beam of light	
razor	an instrument with a sharp blade used for shaving	
reach	to get as far as	**reached** **reaches** **reaching**
reach for	to stretch out to touch something	

read	to say to yourself, or out loud, what you see written	**reader** **reading**
ready	prepared: in a fit state	**readily**
real	not made up: true	**really**
realise	to understand clearly	**realised** **realising**
reap	to cut down and collect a crop	**reaped** **reaper** **reaping**
rear	1. at the back 2. to raise	**reared** **rearing**
reason	1. why something is done 2. common sense	**reasonable**
rebel	someone who fights those in charge	**rebellion**
receipt	a ticket to show that something has been received	
receive	to have something given to you	**received** **receiving**
recent	happening only a little while ago	**recently**
reception	a party held so that people may be received by someone	
recipe	instructions on how to make something to eat or drink	
recite	to say aloud from memory	**recited** **reciting**
reckon	to count up	**reckoned** **reckoning**
recognise	to know someone, or something, again by sight	**recognised** **recognising**
record	1. a round disc played on a record player 2. a note written about anything that has happened	**recording**
recorder	a musical instrument made of wood or plastic	
recover	1. to get something back safely 2. to get well again	**recovered** **recovering** **recovery**

re

recreation	a pleasant way of passing time	
rectangle	an oblong shape with all its angles square	**rectangular**
red	the colour of a tomato or poppy	
reduce	to make smaller	**reduced** **reducing** **reduction**
reed	a tall grass which grows near water	
reel	1. a round, wooden holder on which cotton is wound 2. a Scottish dance	
re-entry	coming back from space into the earth's atmosphere	
referee	someone who sees that the rules are followed in a game	**refereed** **refereeing**
reflect	to throw back rays of light or sound	**reflected** **reflecting** **reflection**
refreshment	something light to eat or drink	
refrigerator	a cold store cupboard for food	
refugee	someone who has to leave his country because of danger	
refuse	1. rubbish 2. to say 'No' when you are asked to do something	**refused** **refusing**
region	a district	
register	a list of names	
regular	at even intervals	**regularly**
rehearse	to practise something for a play or concert	**rehearsal** **rehearsed** **rehearsing**
reign	1. the length of time a king or queen rules 2. to rule	**reigned** **reigning**

reindeer	a deer used for drawing sledges in the cold countries of the north	reindeer
reins	the leather straps that guide a horse	
relation	one who is linked by birth or marriage	
relative	a relation	
relay	a team race in which members of a team each run part of the way	
release	to let go: to set free	**released releasing**
reliable	able to be trusted or relied upon	
religion	belief in god	
rely	to put your trust in someone or something	**relied relies relying**
remain	1. to stay behind 2. to be left over at the end	**remainder remained remaining**
remark	something that is said	
remarkable	unusual: worth mentioning	
remember	to use your memory	**remembered remember- ing**
remind	to jog someone's memory	**reminded reminder reminding**
remove	to take off or to take away	**removal removed removing**
rent	money you pay for living in someone else's house	**rented renting**
repair	to mend	**repaired repairing**
repay	to pay back	**repaid repaying**

repeat	to say, or do, again	**repeated** **repeater** **repeating**
replay	to play again	**replayed** **replaying**
reply	1. an answer 2. to answer	**replies** **replied** **replies** **replying**
report	1. a loud bang 2. the results of your work which are sent to your parents 3. to tell or write about an event	**reported** **reporter** **reporting**
reptile	an animal, such as a snake, whose blood is only as warm as its surroundings	
require	to need	**required** **requiring**
rescue	to save someone or something from danger	**rescued** **rescuer** **rescuing**
reservoir	a place where a large amount of water is stored	
resolution	something you decide that you will try your hardest to do	
respectable	worth admiring	
rest	1. what is left over 2. to lie still and quiet	**rested** **restful** **resting** **restless**
restaurant	a place where you can eat a meal	
result	1. the score at the end of a game 2. the answer to a sum 3. to end in	**resulted** **resulting**
return	to go, or come, back	**returned** **returning**
revenge	something you do to get your own back	

reverse	to go backwards	**reversed** **reversing**
revolver	a small gun which fires several shots without re-loading	
reward	1. a prize for something done well 2. to give someone a reward	**rewarded** **rewarding**
rheumatism	a lasting pain in your bones or muscles	
rhinoceros	a very large, thick-skinned animal with a horn on its nose	**rhinoceroses**
rhubarb	a garden plant, with thick, red juicy stalks which can be cooked and eaten	
rhyme	words which end with the same sound rhyme	
rhythm	a regular beat in music or poetry	
ribbon	a long narrow strip of material	
rice	the seeds of the rice plant, which are an important food in many countries	
rich	wealthy	**richer** **richest** **richly**
riddle	a puzzle	
ride	to sit on something and be carried along	**ridden** **rider** **riding** **rode**
ridge	the line where two slopes meet	
ridiculous	very silly	
rifle	a gun with a long barrel	
right	1. correct 2. the opposite side to the left	
rind	the outside skin	

ring	1. a circle	
	2. a circle of metal worn on the finger	
	3. the sound made by a bell	**rang**
	4. to make a bell sound	**ringing**
		rung
ringlet	a curl of hair	
rinse	to wash out soap or dirt with clean water	**rinsed** **rinsing**
rip	to tear something	**ripped** **ripping**
ripe	ready to be eaten	
rise	1. an increase, usually in wages or prices	**risen** **rising**
	2. to get up, or stand up	**rose**
	3. to go up in the air	
risk	1. a danger	**risked**
	2. to take a chance	**risking** **risky**
river	a large stream flowing towards the sea	
road	a hard track for cars and lorries	**roadside**
roam	to stroll or wander about	**roamed** **roaming**
roar	1. a loud deep noise, like the noise a lion makes	**roared** **roaring**
	2. to make a very loud noise	
roast	to cook anything at an open fire or in an oven	**roasted** **roasting**
rob	to steal by force	**robbed** **robber** **robbing**
robbery	stealing by force	**robberies**
robin	a little bird with a red breast	
robot	a machine that seems to act like a real person	
rock	1. stone	**rocked**
	2. to sway gently backwards and forwards	**rockery** **rocking** **rocky**

rocket	1. a firework which shoots up in the air 2. a tube-shaped machine which is driven along by a jet of gases and which travels over great distances
rode	(Turpin *rode* his horse to York)
rogue	a rascal: someone who cheats and is a bad person
roll	1. anything wrapped round to make a tube-shape **rolled roller** 2. a list of names, such as a **rolling** school register 3. to turn over and over
roof	the covering on top of a house
rook	a large black bird with a **rookery** hoarse cry
room	1. one of the parts of a build- **roomy** ing 2. enough space to hold any-thing
root	the underground part of a **rooted** plant
rope	a thick, strong cord **roped**
rose	1. a plant with a prickly stem **rosy** and sweet-smelling flowers 2. (The kite *rose* high into the air)
rot	to go bad **rotted rotten rotting**
rotate	to turn like a wheel **rotated rotating rotation**
rough	1. not smooth or level **roughly** 2. rude: not gentle 3. stormy
round	1. a part of a boxing match 2. shaped like a ring or like a ball 3. on every side of some-thing: around

roundabout
1. a fairground machine with wooden horses or cars going round in a circle
2. a circle of road to help traffic where several roads meet

route
a path or road from one place to another

row
1. a line of people or things
2. a loud quarrel
3. to move a boat through water by using oars — **rowed** **rowing**

royal
to do with a king or queen — **royalty**

rub
to press and slide two things against each other — **rubbed** **rubbing**

rubber
1. the sap of the rubber tree from which tyres, balls and football bladders are made
2. a soft piece of rubber to clean off pencil marks

rubbish
anything which has no use: litter

ruby
a red precious stone — **rubies**

rucksack
a bag carried on the back, usually by climbers or hikers

rudder
the upright, movable blade which steers an aeroplane or boat

rude
bad-mannered: rough — **rudely**

rugby football
rugger } a winter game played with an oval leather ball

ruin
1. a tumble-down building
2. to spoil or destroy someone or something — **ruined** **ruining**

rule
1. an order which you must obey: a law
2. to govern like a king or queen
3. to draw a straight line using a ruler — **ruled** **ruling**

ruler	1. a length of wood or metal for measuring and drawing straight lines 2. someone who rules over other people
rumour	news which spreads quickly without anyone being sure that it is true
run	1. scored by a batsman in a game of cricket **ran** 2. to move along quickly **runner** **running**
rung	1. a step on a ladder 2. (The school bell is *rung* every morning)
runway	the track on an airfield where aircraft land and take off

rush	1. a plant that grows in wet places, used for making mats and baskets **rushes**
	    rushed
	    rushes
	2. to dash forward at a great speed **rushing**

rust	1. a reddish-brown coat that forms on some metals after they have been left wet **rusted**
	    rusting
	    rusty
	2. to become covered with rust

rye	a grain used for food

S

sabotage	to damage something on purpose **sabotaged**
	    sabotaging
	    saboteur

sack	a large, strong bag, made of coarse cloth or thick paper

sad	unhappy: full of sorrow **sadder**
	    saddest
	    sadly
	    sadness

saddle	a seat for the rider of a horse or bicycle	
safe	1. free from harm 2. a strong cupboard in which money is kept safely	**safely** **safer** **safest** **safety**
said	(Mary *said* that she was going home at tea-time)	
sail	1. a sheet of cloth on a ship's mast to catch the wind 2. to travel in a boat or by ship	**sailed** **sailing**
sailor	one of a ship's crew	
saint	a very holy person	
salad	a mixture of vegetables or fruit, which is eaten cold	
sale	when things are sold cheaply	
salmon	a fish with pink flesh	**salmon**
salt	the mineral which gives sea-water its taste	**salted** **salty**
salute	to put your right hand to your forehead as a way of greeting	**saluted** **saluting**
same	exactly alike	
sand	powdered rock found on beaches and in deserts	**sandy**
sandal	a light open shoe with straps	
sandwich	meat, or other food, between two slices of bread	**sandwiches**
sang	(The boys *sang* the hymns well)	
sank	(The boat *sank* to the bottom of the sea)	
sardine	a small fish, usually sold in a tin	
sash	a waist or shoulder band, made of cloth or ribbon	**sashes**
satchel	a shoulder-bag, usually made of leather, for carrying books to school	

satellite	1. a small planet which goes round and round a larger one 2. an artificial object which travels in outer space round the earth
satin	a kind of shining silk cloth
satisfy	to please somebody by doing what is necessary **satisfaction** **satisfactory** **satisfied** **satisfies** **satisfying**
Saturday	the last day of the week
sauce	a liquid served with food to make it tastier **saucy**
saucepan	a long-handled metal pot, used for cooking
saucer	a small, shallow plate for a cup to stand on
sausage	minced meat in a skin case
savage	1. a wild or fierce person **savagely** 2. wild: fierce
save	1. to rescue someone from danger **saved** **saving** 2. to keep something so that you can use it later on
saw	1. a metal blade with teeth for cutting **sawdust** **sawed** 2. to cut with a saw **sawing** 3. (Peter looked out of the **sawn** window and *saw* his brother fall over)
saxophone	a musical wind instrument
say	to speak **said** **saying**
scab	a dry crust which forms over a cut in the skin
scald	1. the mark on your skin **scalded** caused by burning yourself **scalding** with steam or very hot liquid 2. to burn yourself with steam or very hot liquid

scale	1. a weighing machine	
	2. a set of notes in music	
	3. one of the horny discs that protect the skin of fish and snakes	
scalene	a triangle with none of its sides or angles equal	
scar	the mark left after a burn, cut or scratch has healed	**scarred**
scarce	1. less than is needed	**scarcely**
	2. hard to find	**scarcity**
scare	to frighten	**scarecrow**
		scared
		scaring
scarf	a long strip of woollen material to wear round your neck for warmth	**scarves**
scarlet	bright red	
scatter	1. to throw around	**scattered**
	2. to move quickly in all directions	**scattering**
scene	1. a view	**scenery**
	2. the place where something has happened	
	3. a part of a stage play	
scent	a smell, usually pleasant	**scented**
scholar	someone who learns	**scholarship**
school	a place where children or students are taught	
schooner	a kind of large sailing boat	
science	things we know which have been found out by experiments	**scientific**
		scientist
scissors	two blades joined together, with handles to move them, for cutting	
scold	to grumble at someone for what they have done	**scolded**
		scolding
scone	a small, soft sort of cake, often spread with butter	

scooter   a flat board on two wheels with a handlebar, which is pushed along with one foot

scorch   1. a brown mark on something made by burning it slightly **scorches**
                 2. to mark by scorching **scorched**
                 scorches
                 scorching

score   1. the number of goals, runs or points made in a game **scored**
                 scorer
                 2. twenty: 20 **scoring**
                 3. to get goals, runs or points in games

scout   1. a soldier sent out to spy on the enemy **scouted**
                 scouting
                 2. someone in the Scouts **scoutmaster**

scramble   1. to get over uneven ground using hands as well as feet **scrambled**
                 scrambling
                 2. to rush and push to be the first one to get something

scrap   a small piece: something left over

scrape   to smooth, clean or graze something with a sharp-edged tool **scraped**
                 scraping

scratch   1. a small mark made with something sharp or pointed **scratches**
                 scratched
                 2. to make a scratch **scratches**
                 scratching

scream   1. a loud, shrill cry **screamed**
                 2. to give a loud, shrill cry **screaming**

screech   to give a high-pitched scream **screeched**
                 screeches
                 screeching

screen   1. a partition, which can be folded up and moved
                 2. where you see the picture on a television set or in a cinema

screw	1. a nail with ridges round it, used for fastening pieces of wood together securely 2. a ship's propeller 3. to turn or twist round	**screwdriver** **screwed** **screwing**
scribble	to write carelessly	**scribbled** **scribbling**
scripture(s)	the books of the Bible	
scrub	to rub something with a wet, soapy brush, to make it clean	**scrubbed** **scrubbing**
scullery	a place for washing dishes	**sculleries**
scuttle	a bucket for holding coal	
sea	the salt water that covers about three-quarters of the world	**seagull** **seashore** **seasick** **seaside** **seaweed**
seal	1. an animal which lives both in the sea and on land, and eats fish 2. to fasten something so that it cannot be opened without breaking the fastening	**sealed** **sealing**
seam	the line where two pieces of cloth are sewn together	
search	to hunt for something	**searched** **searches** **searching**
season	spring, summer, autumn or winter	
seat	something to sit on	
seaweed	plants which grow in the sea	
second	1. there are sixty in a minute 2. next after the first	
secret	something you do not want anyone else to know	**secretly**
secure	firmly fixed: safe	
see	1. to look at 2. to understand	**saw** **seeing** **seen**

seed	a tiny grain made by a plant which will grow into another plant of the same kind	
seek	to look for	**seeking** **sought**
seem	to appear to be	**seemed** **seeming**
seesaw	a balanced plank, with a seat at each end, which can be made to rock up and down	
seize	to grab quickly	**seized** **seizing**
seldom	not often	
selfish	thinking too much about yourself and what you want	**selfishly**
sell	to give something in exchange for money	**selling** **sold**
semi-	half	
send	to start someone or something on the way	**sending** **sent**
senior	an older person: older	
sense	1. (He lost his *sense* of smell when he had a cold) 2. (There is no *sense* in wasting time)	**senseless**
sensible	showing good sense: wise	
sent	(The girl was *sent* to see the headmaster)	
sentence	1. a set of words that make complete sense 2. a punishment given by a judge	
sentry	a person who keeps guard	**sentries**
separate	1. not joined to anything: apart 2. to part, or cut off anything	**separated** **separately** **separating**
September	the ninth month of the year	
septic	festered: gone bad because of germs and dirt	

sergeant	1. a soldier, with three stripes on the sleeve, in charge of other soldiers 2. a police officer
serial	a story seen or heard one part at a time
serious	1. important and needing attention: grave **seriously** 2. quiet and thoughtful: not joking
sermon	a talk by a preacher, usually in church
serpent	another name for a snake
servant	someone who is paid to work in a house
serve	1. to sell things in a shop **served** 2. to give out helpings of food **server** at the table **service** 3. to do work for someone **serving**
serviette	a piece of cloth or paper to protect your clothes while you are eating
set	1. a group of things which are alike in some way 2. to become firm or hard **setting** 3. to sink below the horizon, as the sun does 4. to put things in their proper place
settee	a long, comfortable seat with a back, for two or more people
settle	1. to stop moving about **settled** 2. to decide how you are go- **settling** ing to deal with something
seven	7 **seventh**
seventeen	17 **seventeenth**
seventy	70 **seventieth**
several	three or four: a small number of

sew	to use a needle and thread	**sewed** **sewing** **sewn**
shabby	nearly worn out	
shade	1. a cover for a light 2. a place without sunlight	**shaded** **shading** **shady**
shadow	a patch of shade caused by anything with a light behind it	
shady	sheltered from the light: cool	
shake	1. to move anything very quickly up and down 2. to tremble	**shaken** **shaker** **shakily** **shaking** **shaky** **shook**
shall	(I *shall* come to school to-morrow)	
shallow	not deep	
shame	a feeling of sorrow when you have done something wrong	
shampoo	1. a liquid soap for washing hair 2. to wash your hair with a shampoo	**shampooed** **shampooing**
shamrock	a plant like clover, which grows mainly in Ireland	
shape	1. the form of something 2. to mould anything	**shaped** **shaping**
share	1. one of the parts into which a thing is divided 2. to divide anything into parts	**shared** **sharing**
shark	a large fish which has rows of sharp teeth	
sharp	1. not blunt: pointed 2. quick to understand or move 3. sour 4. above the note in music	**sharper** **sharpest** **sharply**
sharpen	to make anything sharp	**sharpened** **sharpener** **sharpening**

shatter	to break into small pieces	**shattered** **shattering**
shave	to cut off hair with a razor	**shaved** **shaver** **shaving**
shawl	a piece of cloth to wear round the shoulders	
sheaf	a bundle of papers or corn	**sheaves**
shears	clippers for cutting wool, hedges or grass	
shed	a shelter used for storing things, usually made of wood	
sheep	the animal which gives us mutton and wool	**sheep**
sheet	a large piece of cloth or paper	
shelf	a flat ledge in a cupboard or on the wall, for holding things	**shelves**
shell	a hard cover to protect something soft	**shelled** **shelling**
shelter	a place where you can hide from danger or bad weather	**sheltered** **sheltering**
shepherd	a person who looks after sheep	**shepherdess**
sheriff	the person whose job it was to keep the peace in a county or district	
shield	1. a piece of armour carried on the arm 2. anything used to protect someone from danger	
shift	1. the length of time people work 2. a number of people working together 3. to move something heavy	**shifted** **shifting**
shin	the front of your leg from your knee to your ankle	
shine	1. to glow with light 2. to polish	**shining** **shiny** **shone**
shingle	small stones on a beach	

ship	a large boat for sea voyages	**shipping** **shipwreck** **shipwrecked**
shirt	a piece of clothing of thin cloth	
shiver	1. trembling caused by cold or fear 2. to tremble	**shivered** **shivering**
shock	1. an unpleasant surprise 2. to give someone an unpleasant surprise	**shocked** **shocking**
shoe	a covering worn on the foot	
shone	(The sun *shone* brightly last Sunday)	
shook	(Father *shook* me to wake me)	
shoot	to fire a gun or let loose an arrow	**shooting** **shot**
shop	1. a place where things are sold 2. to go to the shops to buy things	**shopkeeper** **shopped** **shopping**
shore	the land at the edge of the sea or a lake	
short	1. not long in length 2. not lasting long 3. less than is needed: scarce	**shortage** **shorter** **shortest** **shortly**
shorts	very short trousers	
shot	(The farmer *shot* a rabbit with her gun)	**shotgun**
should	(I *should* like to go to the Zoo)	
shoulder	the place where your arm is joined to your body	
shout	1. a loud cry 2. to call out loudly	**shouted** **shouting**
shove	1. a push 2. to push something to move it	**shoved** **shoving**

shovel	1. a spade with curved-up edges 2. to move things using a shovel	**shovelled** **shovelling**
show	1. an entertainment 2. to let something be seen 3. to make something clear by explaining it	**showed** **showing** **shown**
shower	rain falling for only a short time	**showery**
shrimp	a small grey shellfish which turns pink when it is cooked	
shrink	to get smaller	**shrank** **shrinking**
shrub	a plant like a small tree, but with no trunk: a bush	
shunt	to use an engine to push loose wagons and carriages to a different railway line	**shunted** **shunter** **shunting**
shut	1. closed 2. to close anything	**shutting**
sick	ill	**sickly** **sickness**
side	1. an edge or border 2. a group of players in a game	**sideways**
sideboard	a cupboard for holding everything you need to lay a table	
siding	railway lines off the main line where wagons can be parked	
sigh	to take a very deep breath because you are tired or sad	**sighed** **sighing**
sight	1. something you see 2. being able to see 3. to get a view of something	**sighted** **sighting**

sign	1. a mark which has a meaning	**signature**
		signed
	2. a thing or event which tells	**signing**
	you something will happen	
	3. a movement you make to let someone know what you want	
	4. to write your name	
signal	1. a message sent by signs	**signalled**
	2. to send a message by signs	**signalling**
	3. a sign used on a railway	**signalman**
silent	not making any sound	**silence**
		silently
silk	a smooth, soft cloth, made from the thin thread spun by the caterpillar of a silk moth	**silkworm**
		silky
silly	foolish	**sillier**
		silliest
		silliness
silver	1. a shiny, precious metal	**silvery**
	2. the colour of silver	
	3. all the coins which are silver-coloured	
similar	the same, or nearly the same	
simple	1. very easy to do or understand	**simply**
	2. silly: foolish	
since	(I have not been swimming *since* last summer)	
sincere	honest: not pretending	**sincerely**
sing	to make a tune with your voice	**sang**
		singer
		singing
		sung
single	1. one only	
	2. not married	
sink	1. a bowl with a tap and drain in a kitchen	**sank**
		sinking
	2. to fall downwards through water	**sunk**
sip	to drink in small amounts	**sipped**
		sipping

sister (My *sister* and I are the only children my parents have)

sit to be seated — **sat**, **sitting**

six 6 — **sixth**

sixteen 16 — **sixteenth**

sixty 60 — **sixtieth**

size the measurement of anything

skate
1. a blade, or four wheels, fixed on a shoe, so that you can glide or roll along
2. to roll or glide on skates over the ground or on ice

— **skated**, **skater**, **skating**

skeleton the bones in a body

skid to slide suddenly on something smooth or slippery — **skidded**, **skidding**

skill cleverness at doing something — **skilful**, **skilled**

skim
1. to take off anything floating on top of a liquid
2. to glide over something, hardly touching it

— **skimmed**, **skimming**

skin
1. the outer covering on the body of a person or animal
2. the outer covering of fruit
3. to take off skin or peel

— **skinned**, **skinning**

skin-diver someone who dives and swims underwater without a diving suit

skip
1. to jump lightly from one foot to the other
2. to use a skipping rope

— **skipped**, **skipping**

skipper the captain of a boat or ship

skirt a piece of clothing which hangs from the waist

skull the bones of the head

sky the space round the earth, where the clouds float — **skies**

skylark	a small bird which soars very high into the air and sings as it flies
skyscraper	a very tall building
slack	1. loose: not tight **slacked** 2. lazy and careless about **slacker** work **slacking**
slacks	trousers worn by women
slam	to close something with great **slammed** force **slamming**
slant	1. a slope **slanted** 2. to put something with one **slanting** end higher than the other
slap	1. a blow given with an open **slapped** hand **slapping** 2. to smack someone with the flat of your hand
slave	1. a person who belongs to a **slaved** master and who must work **slavery** for him **slaving** 2. to work very hard
sledge	a low carriage with runners **sledging** instead of wheels, which runs smoothly over snow
sleep	1. a rest in which you lose any **sleeping** sense of the things about **sleepless** you **sleepy** 2. to rest your body by sleep- **slept** ing: to be asleep
sleeper	1. someone who is sleeping 2. a heavy piece of wood or concrete to which railway lines are fastened
sleet	snow or hail falling with rain
sleeve	the part of your clothes which covers your arm
slice	1. a thin, flat piece which is **sliced** cut off something **slicing** 2. to cut anything in slices

slide	1. a hair clip	slid
	2. to slip along over something smooth, such as ice	sliding
slight	1. not big	slightly
	2. not important	
slim	not fat	slimmer
		slimmest
slime	very fine slippery mud	slimy
slip	1. a small mistake	slipped
	2. to slide a little way by accident	slippery
		slipping
	3. to go quietly and quickly	
slippers	soft comfortable shoes to wear indoors	
slit	1. a long thin cut or opening in anything	slitting
	2. to make a long cut in something	
slope	slanting ground	sloped
		sloping
slot	a narrow opening or groove in something	slot-machine
slow	1. behind in time	slowed
	2. taking a long time to do something	slower
		slowest
		slowing
		slowly
slush	1. soft mud	slushy
	2. half-melted snow	
sly	cunning: crafty	slyly
smack	1. a quick blow from an open hand	smacked
		smacking
	2. to slap anyone with the flat part of your hand	
small	little in size or amount: not large	smaller
		smallest
smart	1. well-dressed	smarted
	2. quick and sharp	smarter
	3. to feel a sharp, tingling pain	smartest
		smarting
		smartly

smash	1. a collision: a crash 2. to dash something to pieces	**smashes** **smashed** **smashes** **smashing**
smell	1. the scent of anything 2. to notice the scent of any- thing 3. to have a scent	**smelling** **smelly** **smelt**
smile	1. a happy look 2. to look pleased and happy	**smiled** **smiling**
smog	smoke and fog together	
smoke	1. the fumes that come from something burning 2. to give out smoke 3. to use a cigarette, pipe or cigar	**smoked** **smoker** **smoking** **smoky**
smooth	1. without any roughness: level 2. to make something level and smooth	**smoothed** **smoother** **smoothest** **smoothing** **smoothly**
smudge	1. a smear: a dirty mark 2. to make a dirty mark on something	**smudged** **smudging** **smudgy**
smuggle	to take goods into or out of a country in secret, to avoid paying a tax on them	**smuggled** **smuggler** **smuggling**
snail	a little creature, with a shell on its back, which crawls very slowly	
snake	an animal like a large worm	
snap	1. a sudden sharp or cracking sound 2. to break suddenly 3. to try to bite something or somebody 4. to speak sharply and angrily	**snapped** **snappily** **snapping** **snappy** **snapshot**
snatch	to grab something quickly	**snatched** **snatches** **snatching**

sneeze	the sudden noise you make when something tickles your nose	**sneezed** **sneezing**
sniff	to breathe air in quickly through your nose	**sniffed** **sniffing**
snore	to breathe noisily while you are asleep	**snored** **snoring**
snow	1. soft white flakes of frozen rain, which sometimes fall on a cold day 2. to fall as snow	**snowball** **snowbound** **snowed** **snowflake** **snowing** **snowman** **snowstorm** **snowy**
soak	1. to leave something lying in liquid 2. to make something very wet	**soaked** **soaking**
soap	something made from fat and used for washing	**soap-** **powder** **soapsuds** **soapy**
soccer	football played with a round ball	
sock	a short stocking: a covering for the foot and ankle	
sofa	a long, soft seat with a back and arms, on which two or three people can sit	
soft	1. not hard 2. easily bent or squashed 3. gentle and quiet	**softer** **softest** **softly**
soil	1. the ground in which plants grow 2. to make something dirty	**soiled** **soiling**
sold	(My mother *sold* a book for 5p)	
soldier	a person in the army	

sole	1. the bottom of your foot	**soled**
	2. the bottom part of a shoe	**soling**
	3. a flat fish which can be eaten	
	4. only	
solid	1. firm and not changing its shape	
	2. not hollow	
solve	to work out the answer to a problem	**solution**
		solved
		solving
some	an amount	**somebody**
		someone
		something
		sometimes
		somewhere
somersault	to turn head over heels	**somer-saulted**
		somer-saulting
son	the boy child of a mother and father	
song	1. words set to music	
	2. sweet sounds made by a bird	
soon	before long: shortly	**sooner**
		soonest
soot	specks of partly burnt coal which smoke leaves in a chimney	**sooty**
sore	1. a painful spot on your skin	**soreness**
	2. tender and painful	
sorrow	sadness	**sorrowful**
sorry	sad because you have done wrong, or because of something that has happened: regretful	
sort	1. a kind	**sorted**
	2. to separate things into groups	**sorting**

sought	(John *sought* his toys but could not find them)	
soul	the part of a person that is thought to live on after death	
sound	1. something that we can hear 2. in a good state: healthy 3. to make a noise	**sounded** **sounding** **sound-proof**
soup	liquid food made by boiling vegetables or meat	
sour	an unripe, acid taste	
source	the place where a river or stream starts	
south	the opposite to north	**southern**
souvenir	a thing kept to remind you of a person or a place	
sow	1. a female pig 2. to plant seeds	**sowed** **sowing** **sown**
space	1. the distance between things 2. far from the earth, where there is no air	**space-ship**
spade	a sharp-edged blade on a handle, used for digging	
span	the distance between the tips of your thumb and little finger when your hand is stretched out	
spaniel	a long-eared dog with a silky coat	
spanner	a tool for turning bolts or nuts	
spare	extra: not needed	
spark	a tiny piece thrown out from something burning: a flash	**sparking**
sparkle	to glitter or glisten	**sparkled** **sparkler** **sparkling**
sparrow	a small brownish-grey bird	
speak	to talk	**speaker** **speaking** **spoke**

spear	a weapon with a long handle and a sharp-pointed end	
special	for a particular use	**specialist** **specially**
speck	a tiny piece, often of dirt	**speckled**
spectacles	glasses worn to help your sight	
spectator	someone who watches a show, a game or anything happening	
speech	1. a talk to an audience 2. the power to speak	**speeches** **speechless**
speed	1. the rate at which something moves 2. quickness 3. to move very fast	**speeded** **speeding** **speedy**
speedometer	an instrument in a car to show how fast it is travelling	
speedway	a race-track for motor-cycles or cars	
spell	1. words supposed to have magic power 2. to arrange letters to make words	**spelled** **spelling** **spelt**
spend	1. to pay out money 2. to use up time in doing something	**spending** **spent**
sphere	a ball shape	**spherical**
spice	something like pepper or curry, for making food more tasty	
spider	a creature with eight legs, which spins a web to catch insects	
spill	to tip over	**spilled** **spilling** **spilt**
spin	1. to twist into threads 2. to turn round and round	**spinning** **spun**
spiral	a screw-shaped curve	

spite	trying to hurt someone by cruel words or behaviour	**spiteful** **spitefully**
splash	to scatter water about	**splashed** **splashes** **splashing**
splash-down	to land in the water, as some space capsules do	
splendid	gorgeous: magnificent: showy	**splendidly**
splinter	a sharp piece broken off something	**splintered**
split	1. a long tear or crack 2. to tear or break something	**splitting**
spoil	to damage or destroy something	**spoiled** **spoiling** **spoilt**
spoke	1. a bar or strong wire which holds the rim of a wheel to the centre 2. (When the teacher *spoke* we all listened)	**spoken**
sponge	1. a soft thing which soaks up water and is used in the bath 2. to wash or wipe something with a sponge	**sponged** **sponging** **spongy**
spoon	something used for eating or stirring soft food	**spoonful**
sport	a game such as football, racing or fishing	**sports- jacket** **sportsman**
spot	1. a stain or mark 2. to see something	**spotless** **spotted** **spotter** **spotting**
spout	a tube with a shaped mouthpiece for liquid to run through	
sprain	1. a twisted muscle 2. to harm a muscle by twisting it	**sprained** **spraining**
sprang	(The tiger *sprang* out from its hiding-place)	

spray	1. a shower of tiny drops of water 2. to shoot a liquid out from anything, in a shower	**sprayed** **sprayer** **spraying**
spread	to make something cover a greater surface, by unrolling, smearing or flattening it out	**spreading**
spring	1. water flowing out from the ground 2. a coil of metal which goes back into shape after it has been bent or pressed 3. to jump or leap	**sprang** **springing** **sprung**
spring	the season between winter and summer	
sprinkle	to scatter lightly	**sprinkled** **sprinkling**
sprint	to run as fast as you can for a short distance	**sprinted** **sprinter** **sprinting**
spun	(The spider *spun* its web and caught a fly)	
spy	1. someone who secretly watches an enemy 2. to watch secretly	**spies** **spied** **spies** **spy-catcher** **spying**
squabble	to quarrel noisily	**squabbled** **squabbling**
square	1. a shape with four straight, equal sides and four equal angles 2. an open space in a town	
squash	1. a fruit drink 2. to squeeze or crush	**squashes** **squashed** **squashes** **squashing**
squeak	to make a short, sharp, high sound	**squeaked** **squeaking**
squeal	to make a long sharp cry, usually of pain or fright	**squealed** **squealing**

squeeze	to press or crush	**squeezed** **squeezing**
squirrel	a small animal with a bushy tail	
squirt	to shoot water out in a thin stream	**squirted** **squirter** **squirting**
stab	to wound someone with a pointed weapon	**stabbed** **stabbing**
stable	a shelter for a horse	
stack	1. a pile of things one on top of another 2. to make a pile of things	**stacked** **stacking**
staff	1. a strong stick 2. a number of people who work together, as in a school or office	**staff-room**
stag	a male deer	
stage	the platform on which plays are acted	
stagger	to walk in a very unsteady way	**staggered** **staggering**
stain	1. a dirty mark not easy to remove 2. a dye for wood	**stained** **staining** **stainless**
stairs	a number of steps	**staircase**
stake	a post fixed in the ground	
stale	not fresh: old	
stalk	1. the stem of a flower or plant 2. to follow an animal in order to catch or watch it	**stalked** **stalking**
stall	1. a shop in a market 2. a seat near the stage in a theatre	
stamp	1. a piece of paper to stick on letters or parcels so that you can send them by post 2. to stick on a stamp 3. to bang your foot on the ground	**stamped** **stamping**

stand	1. raised seats, usually under cover, from which people watch a game or races	**standing** **stood**
	2. to be upright on your feet	
	3. to suffer without complaining	
star	1. a large object in space, seen as a point of light in the sky at night	
	2. a famous actor or actress	
starch	1. a white powder used with water for stiffening clothes	**starched** **starches**
	2. to stiffen clothes with starch	**starching** **starchy**
stare	to look hard at anything with wide-open eyes	**stared** **staring**
starling	a bird with dark, speckled feathers	
start	to begin	**started** **starter** **starting**
starve	to suffer or die because of lack of food	**starvation** **starved** **starving**
station	1. a place where trains or 'buses stop	
	2. a building for police officers or fire fighters	
stationary	standing still	
stationery	materials for writing	
statue	a carving in wood or stone, usually of a person or an animal	
stay	to stop in one place for a time	**stayed** **staying**
steady	1. firm: not rocking or moving	**steadily**
	2. (Joan is a *steady* worker. She is neither fast nor slow)	
steak	a thick slice of meat	

steal	to take something which is not yours	**stealing** **stole** **stolen**
steam	1. the cloud you see coming from boiling water 2. to give off steam	**steamed** **steaming**
steamer	a ship driven by steam	
steel	a very strong metal made from iron	
steep	sloping very sharply	**steeper** **steepest** **steeply**
steeple	a pointed tower	
steer	to guide anything	**steered** **steering**
stem	a stalk	
step	1. one pace with your foot 2. one part of a staircase 3. to take one pace	**stepped** **stepping**
stern	1. the back end of a ship 2. strict: severe	
stew	1. a dish of vegetables and meat, which have been cooked together in water 2. to cook something slowly in boiling water	**stewed** **stewing**
stick	1. a thin bit of wood 2. to fix something with paste or glue	**sticking** **sticky** **stuck**
stiff	1. cannot be bent easily 2. hard or difficult	**stiffen** **stiffly** **stiffness**
stile	a fence with a step on each side	
still	1. not moving 2. in spite of something: yet	
stilt	a pole with a step at the side, used in pairs for walking above the ground	

sting	1. a small amount of poison pricked into your skin by an insect or plant 2. the part of an insect or plant that causes a sting 3. to prick a small amount of poison into the skin	**stinging** **stung**
stir	1. to mix something, usually with a spoon 2. to move	**stirred** **stirring**
stitch	1. a thread put through cloth with a needle, or a loop made with wool in knitting 2. to sew with thread	**stitches** **stitched** **stitches** **stitching**
stocking	a covering for the foot and leg, usually made of nylon	
stoke	to put fuel on a fire	**stoked** **stoker** **stoking**
stole	(The thief *stole* the money from the shop)	**stolen**
stomach	the part of the body where food is partly dissolved	
stone	a piece of rock: a pebble	
stood	(We *stood* at the roadside to watch the carnival go by)	
stool	a small seat without a back or arms	
stoop	to bend the body forward	**stooped** **stooping**
stop	1. a stopping place 2. to bring someone or something to a standstill 3. to halt: to end	**stoppage** **stopped** **stopping**
stopper	a plug or cork for a bottle	
store	1. a place where things can be kept until they are wanted 2. a large shop selling many different things 3. to put a thing away until it is needed	**stored** **storing**

storey	a floor of a building, and the rooms in it	
stork	a bird with a long beak, legs and neck	
storm	very bad weather with heavy rain, strong winds, thunder and lightning or snow	**stormy**
story	a tale	**stories**
stout	1. strongly built 2. fat	
stove	a closed-in fire for cooking, or for warming a building	
stowaway	someone who hides in a ship or aircraft, so that he can travel without paying his fare	
straight	1. without a curve or bend 2. honest	**straighten** **straighter** **straightest**
strain	1. to try very hard to do a diffi-cult thing 2. to pull or stretch	**strained** **straining**
strait	a narrow channel of sea	
strange	1. new or not known to you 2. unusual	**strangely** **stranger** **strangest**
stranger	1. someone you do not know 2. a person in a country or town to which he does not belong	
strap	1. a strip of leather or cloth with a buckle 2. to fasten with straps	**strapped** **strapping**
straw	dry stalks of cut corn	
strawberry	a soft, juicy, red fruit, with small yellow seeds on its skin	**strawberries**
stray	to wander from home or lose your way	**strayed** **straying**
stream	a brook: a small river	
stream-lined	smoothly shaped to pass smoothly through air or water	

street	a road with houses or shops	
strength	being strong: power	
stretch	to pull out to make something longer	**stretched** **stretches** **stretching**
stretcher	a canvas bed for carrying anyone who is ill or injured	
strict	stern	**stricter** **strictest**
strike	1. a time when a group of people try to get something they want by refusing to work 2. to hit	**striking** **struck**
string	fine cord: twine	**stringy**
strip	1. a thin, long piece of anything 2. to take the cover off something	**stripped** **stripping**
stripe	a narrow band of colour	**striped**
stroke	1. a movement of the arm 2. a swimming movement 3. to smooth something with the hand	**stroked** **stroking**
stroll	1. a slow pleasant walk 2. to go for a slow walk	**strolled** **strolling**
strong	1. powerful 2. tough: hard to break 3. healthy	**stronger** **strongest** **strongly**
struck	(I cut my head when I *struck* it against the wall)	
struggle	1. to fight with something or someone 2. to try hard	**struggled** **struggling**
stubborn	hard to persuade: unwilling	
stuck	1. glued or pasted 2. not free	
stud	1. a double-headed button for holding a collar in place 2. a nail with a large knob	

study	1. a room for quiet work 2. to read to learn	**studies** **student** **studied** **studies** **studying**
stuff	1. material that anything is made from 2. to fill something tightly	
stuffy	short of fresh air	
stumble	to catch your foot on something and lose your balance	**stumbled** **stumbling**
stump	1. the part of the tree still in the ground after the tree has been cut down 2. one of three wooden sticks which make a wicket for cricket	**stumped** **stumping**
stung	(John screamed when he was *stung* by a wasp)	
stupid	silly: foolish: dull	**stupidity** **stupidly**
stutter	to stumble over words while trying to speak: to stammer	**stuttered** **stuttering**
sty	1. the building where a pig is kept 2. a painful swelling on an eyelid	**sties** or **styes**
subject	1. the thing you write, read and learn about 2. a person ruled by a king or queen	
submarine	a warship that can sail both above and below the surface of the sea	
submerge	to go down under the water	**submerged** **submerging**
subtract	to take away	**subtracted** **subtraction**
suburb	a district on the edge of a town or city	**suburban**

subway	a passageway under a busy road
succeed	1. to do well at what you set out to do **succeeded** **succeeding** 2. to come after, and take the place of, somebody **succession**
success	a thing or person that turns out well **successes** **successful**
such	(It was *such* a beautiful day that we went swimming)
suck	to draw something into your mouth **sucked** **sucking**
sudden	happening quickly and without warning **suddenly**
suet	solid fat of cattle or sheep used in cooking
suffer	to feel pain or sorrow **suffered** **suffering**
sufficient	enough
sugar	something used to sweeten food
suggest	to offer someone an idea or plan **suggested** **suggesting** **suggestion**
suit	1. a set of matching clothes **suited** 2. to fit in with your ideas or wishes **suiting** 3. to go well with someone's looks or colouring
suitable	just right **suitability**
sulk	to show you are cross by refusing to speak to people **sulked** **sulking** **sulky**
sultana	one kind of grape that has been partly dried and is used in cakes
summer	the season between spring and autumn

summit	the top, usually of a mountain	
sun	the star that gives us light and warmth	**sunburnt** **sunflower** **sunlight** **sunny** **sunrise** **sunset** **sunshine** **sunstroke**
Sunday	the first day of the week	
sung	(The song was *sung* well)	
sunk	(The ship was *sunk* when it hit the rocks)	
supermarket	a large shop where customers usually serve themselves, and pay as they leave	
supersonic	travelling faster than sound	
supper	the last meal of the day	
support	1. anything which helps to hold something up or which bears a mass (weight) 2. to hold something up	**supported** **supporter** **supporting**
suppose	to accept as likely	**supposed** **supposing**
sure	certain: without any doubts	
surf	large waves breaking on the shore	
surface	the top or outside of something	
surgery	the room where a doctor sees her patients	**surgeries**
surname	your family name	
surprise	1. something unexpected 2. to give someone a surprise	**surprised** **surprising**
surrender	to give up	**surrendered** **surrendering**
surround	to be all round something or someone	**surrounded** **surrounding**

suspect	1. someone who is believed to have done something wrong 2. to have a feeling that someone has done something wrong	**suspected** **suspecting**
suspicious	1. doubting whether something is true: not trusting 2. not to be trusted	**suspiciously**
swallow	1. a bird with pointed wings and a forked tail 2. to let something pass down your throat	**swallowed** **swallowing**
swam	(The sailor *swam* to the raft)	
swamp	a boggy piece of land	**swamped** **swamping** **swampy**
swan	a large, white bird with a very long neck	
swarm	a crowd of bees, all close together	**swarmed** **swarming**
sway	to rock from side to side	**swayed** **swaying**
swear	1. to take an oath 2. to use bad language	**swearing** **swore** **sworn**
sweat	1. the wetness that comes on your skin when you are hot 2. to become wet through being hot	**sweated** **sweating**
sweater	a woollen jersey or pullover	
sweep	1. a person who sweeps chimneys 2. to use a brush or broom	**sweeper** **sweeping** **swept**
sweet	1. (I buy *sweets* with my pocket money) 2. with a sugary taste 3. pleasant to hear or see	**sweeter** **sweetest** **sweetly**
swell	1. to get bigger 2. to get louder	**swelled** **swelling** **swollen**

swept	(Jim *swept* up all the dust from the floor)	
swerve	to turn to one side suddenly	**swerved** **swerving**
swift	1. a bird like a swallow 2. quick	**swifter** **swiftest** **swiftly**
swim	to move through water, using your arms and legs	**swam** **swimmer** **swimming** **swum**
swing	1. a seat hanging from ropes 2. to move backwards and for- wards in a curve	**swinging** **swung**
switch	1. a thing for turning elec- tricity on or off 2. to use a switch for turning electricity on or off 3. to change over	**switches** **switched** **switches** **switching**
swollen	(My leg was *swollen* where it had been hit)	
swoop	to dive downwards	**swooped** **swooping**
sword	a sharp-pointed weapon with a long, thin blade	
swore	(I *swore* to keep the secret)	
sworn	(The robber had *sworn* to get her revenge)	
swung	(The monkey *swung* from one branch to another)	
sycamore	a tree with broad five-pointed leaves	
symmetry	having the two halves the same shape and size	**symmetric** **symmetrical**
syrup	a sugary liquid	

t

table
a piece of furniture with a flat surface which stands on legs
tablecloth
tablespoon

tack
1. a long loose sewing-stitch
2. a short, flat-topped nail
3. to fasten something down with a tack or tacking-stitch
tacked
tacking

tackle
1. to try to do something that is awkward
2. to try to get the ball away from another player in a game
tackled
tackling

tadpole
a partly-grown toad, frog or newt

tail
the part which hangs or sticks out from the back of an animal

tailor
a person who makes suits, coats and trousers

take
1. to get hold of: to receive
2. (I *take* my satchel home at night)
taken
taking
took

tale
a story

talk
1. a speech
2. to speak
talkative
talked
talking

tall
high
taller
tallest

tame
1. not wild or fierce
2. to make obedient
tamed
tamely
tamer
tamest
taming

tangerine
a kind of small orange

tangle
twisted together in a muddle

tank
1. a large holder for liquids or gases
2. an armoured car with tracks instead of wheels

tanker a ship for carrying oil or other liquids

tap
1. a pipe or hole which can be **tapped** opened or closed to let **tapping** liquid through
2. to hit gently

tape a narrow strip of material, usually cloth

taper to get thinner towards the end **tapered** **tapering**

tape recorder a machine that records and plays back sound

tar
1. a dark-coloured sticky **tarred** liquid, taken from coal or **tarring** wood
2. to put tar on

target something to aim at

tart
1. a pie with fruit in it, or pastry with jam on it
2. sour in taste

tartan woollen cloth with a checked pattern

task a piece of work to be done

taste
1. the flavour of food **tasted**
2. to notice the flavour of any- **tasteless** thing put in your mouth **tasting** **tasty**

taught (We are *taught* by a teacher)

tax money paid to the govern- **taxes** ment

taxi a car for hiring

tea a drink made from the young **teapot** leaves of the tea plant **teaspoon** **teaspoonful**

teach to explain how to do some- **taught** thing: to give lessons **teacher** **teaches** **teaching**

team a number of people, or animals, working together

tear	1. a drop of salty water from your eye 2. to rip	**tearing** **tore** **torn**
tease	to annoy somebody in fun	**teased** **teasing**
teeth	(We clean our *teeth* after meals)	
telegram	a written message sent very quickly by the Post Office in the past	
telephone	an electrical instrument by means of which sounds are carried by wires over long distances	
telescope	an eye-glass which makes far away things seem near	
television	the sending and receiving of pictures by radio	
tell	to say a message or story to someone	**telling** **told**
temper	1. the sort of mood you are in 2. anger	
temperature	the reading on a thermometer which shows how hot or cold anything is	
tempt	to try to get someone to do something which they ought not to do	**temptation** **tempted** **tempting**
ten	10	**tenth**
tender	1. a railway truck which carries fuel and water for the locomotive 2. soft: not tough 3. loving	
tennis	a game for two or four people, played with rackets and a ball	
tent	a canvas shelter	
term	the time spent in school between holidays	

terminus	the place where a 'bus or train ends its journey	**termini**
terrier	a small dog	
terrify	to fill someone with terror	**terrific** **terrified** **terrifies** **terrifying**
terror	great fear and dread	**terrible** **terribly**
test	1. an examination	**tested**
	2. to try out someone or something	**testing**
than	(Four is bigger *than* three)	
thank	to say you are grateful	**thanked** **thankful** **thankfully** **thanking**
that	1. (He knows *that* I will be late)	
	2. (This is the one *that* I like)	
thatch	a roof of straw or reeds	**thatches** **thatched** **thatching**
thaw	to melt from snow or ice	**thawed** **thawing**
theatre	a place where people watch actors on a stage	
their	belonging to them	
them	(Sally and John were good, so the teacher gave *them* a star)	**themselves**
then	1. at that time	
	2. so after that	
there	in that place	**therefore**
thermometer	an instrument for measuring how hot or cold anything is	
thermos	a special flask that keeps what it holds hot or cold	
these	(*These* books are mine)	

they	(John and Mary were late so *they* ran home)	
thick	1. wide: not thin 2. crowded 3. dense 4. not runny	**thickly** **thickness**
thief	someone who steals	**thieves**
thigh	the top of your leg	
thimble	a finger cover, to help to press a needle through cloth	
thin	not thick: slim	**thinly** **thinner** **thinnest**
thing	any object	
think	1. to use your mind 2. to believe	**thinking** **thought**
third	3rd	
thirst	the feeling you have when you want a drink	**thirsty**
thirteen	13	**thirteenth**
thirty	30	**thirtieth**
this	(*This* pen is better than that one)	
thistle	a plant with prickly leaves and a purple, white or yellow flower	
thorn	the prickle of a bush, plant or tree	**thorny**
those	(*Those* pencils over there have been sharpened)	
thorough	careful: well done	**thoroughly**
though	even if	
thought	1. an idea: something which you think 2. (I *thought* I had finished my work)	**thoughtful** **thoughtless**
thousand	1000	**thousandth**

thread	1. a piece of cotton, wool, nylon, or silk cord, or any fibre 2. to push thread through a hole in anything	**threaded** **threading**
threat	a warning that trouble is coming	
threaten	to say that you will hurt or punish someone	**threatened** **threatening**
three	3	**third**
threw	(Jill *threw* the ball into the air, and John caught it)	
thrill	1. an excited feeling 2. to make someone feel excited	**thrilled** **thrilling**
thriller	an exciting story, usually about crime	
throat	the tube which leads from mouth to stomach	
throb	to beat strongly	**throbbed** **throbbing**
throne	a special chair for a king or queen, or very important person	
through	from one end to the other	
throw	to fling something through the air	**threw** **throwing** **thrown**
thrush	a brown bird with a sweet song	**thrushes**
thud	a dull, bumping sound	
thumb	the short, thick finger, nearest the wrist	
thump	to beat with the fist	**thumped** **thumping**
thunder	the loud noise that follows lightning	**thunder- storm** **thundery**
Thursday	the fifth day of the week	

tick	1. the clicking sound made by a clock	**ticked**
		ticking
	2. a mark to show that your work has been checked	
ticket	a card giving you the right to a place on a 'bus or train or to watch something	
tickle	to touch someone lightly to make him laugh	**tickled**
		tickling
		ticklish
tide	the rise and fall of the sea twice daily	
tidy	1. neat	**tidied**
	2. to arrange anything neatly	**tidier**
		tidies
		tidiest
		tidily
		tidiness
		tidying
tie	1. a band round the neck, which ties in front	**tied**
		ties
	2. to fasten with string or ribbon	**tying**
	3. to have the same score	
tiger	a large, striped animal like a fierce cat	**tigress**
tight	fitting closely	**tighter**
		tightest
		tightly
		tights
tile	a thin slab, usually made of baked clay	**tiled**
till	1. a money-drawer in a shop	
	2. up to: as late as	
	3. to dig land	**tilled**
tilt	to slope or slant anything	**tilted**
		tilting
timber	wood	
time	1. the hour of the day	**timed**
	2. to find out how long it takes to do something	**timetable**
		timing
	3. (We had a good *time* today)	

timid	shy: easily made afraid	**timidly**
tingle	to have a prickling or stinging feeling	**tingled** **tingling**
tinned	in a sealed tin	
tinsel	shiny metal threads or strips used for decoration	
tiny	very small	**tinier** **tiniest**
tip	1. the pointed end of anything 2. a small gift of money given to someone who has been helpful 3. to tilt: to overturn	**tipped** **tipping**
tiptoe	to walk on your toes	**tiptoed** **tiptoeing**
tire	to make weary	**tired** **tiring**
tissue	a very thin, soft paper	
title	1. the name of anything which is written 2. a name to show a person's rank	**titled**
toad	a creature like a frog, but with a drier skin	
toast	1. bread browned by heat 2. to make bread brown by heating it	**toasted** **toaster** **toasting**
tobacco	the leaves of the tobacco plant which are used for smoking	**tobacconist**
toboggan	a sledge for sliding on snow	
today	this day	
toe	one of the five tips of the foot	
toffee	a sweet made from butter, sugar and treacle	
together	1. with something or someone else 2. at the same time	
toilet	a lavatory or wash place	
told	(I *told* him to sit)	

to

tomato	a soft fruit with a red skin	**tomatoes**
tomorrow	the day after today	
tongs	a kind of pincer, used for picking up coal	
tongue	the loose piece of flesh in the mouth which helps you to eat and speak	
tonight	after this evening	
tonsils	two glands at the back of the mouth to protect the throat	**tonsillitis**
too	1. also 2. more than enough	
took	(Eric *took* a present to his friend)	
tool	something to work with	
tooth	a bone which grows in your jaw for biting and chewing	**teeth** **toothache**
torch	a light carried in the hand	**torches**
tore	(Jane *tore* her dress on a nail)	
torn	(Jane's dress was *torn* by a nail)	
tortoise	a reptile, with a hard shell, which moves very slowly	
torture	to be cruel to someone by causing great pain	**tortured** **torturing**
toss	to throw into the air	**tossed** **tosses** **tossing**
total	1. the complete amount 2. complete 3. to add up to	**totalled** **totalling**
touch	1. to feel 2. to be so near that there is no space between	**touched** **touches** **touching**
tough	hard to break or cut	
tow	to pull along	**towed** **towing**
towards	in the direction of	

towel	a thick cotton or linen cloth for drying your body	
tower	a tall, narrow building	
town	a large number of houses and other buildings	
toy	something to play with	
trace	1. a mark left behind	**traced**
	2. to copy something by following its shape on thin paper that is placed over it	**tracing**
track	1. marks left by someone or something as he or it passed	**tracked** **tracking**
	2. a rough path	
	3. railway lines	
	4. to follow a track	
tractor	a powerful machine used on farms for pulling heavy loads	
trade	1. buying and selling things	**traded**
	2. a job needing skilled hands	**tradesman**
	3. to buy and sell things	**trading**
traffic	people or goods coming and going by road, rail, sea or air	
trail	1. a track left by something as it passed by	**trailed** **trailer**
	2. to drag something along	**trailing**
train	1. railway carriages drawn by an engine	**trained** **trainer**
	2. to prepare by practising	**training**
traitor	someone who betrays his friends or his country	
tramp	a wandering beggar	
transfer	1. a picture or pattern you can stick on to something else	
	2. to move something or somebody to another place	**transferred** **transferring**
transfusion	passing blood from one person to another	
transistor	1. a thing used to increase an electrical current	
	2. a portable radio	

transparent   letting light pass through   **trans-parency**

transplant   to take up or out and plant in another place   **trans-planted trans-planting**

trap
1. (I set a *trap* to catch mice)   **trapped**
2. a two-wheeled, open carriage   **trapping**
3. to catch a person or animal, usually by a trick

trapdoor   a door in a floor, stage or ceiling

travel   to make a journey   **travelled traveller travelling**

trawler   a fishing boat which drags its net

tray   a flat board with raised edges

treacle   syrup made from sugar

tread   to walk   **treading trod trodden**

treason   betraying your country

treasure   something worth a great deal of money   **treasurer treasury**

treat
1. anything that gives you much pleasure   **treated treating**
2. to look after   **treatment**

tree   a large plant with a thick wood stem and branches

tremble   to shiver with fear or excitement   **trembled trembling**

trench   a long narrow ditch, dug in the ground   **trenches**

trespass   to go on someone else's property without permission   **trespassed trespasser trespassing**

trial	a way of testing something or somebody	
triangle	1. the shape made by joining three straight lines 2. a musical percussion instrument	
trick	1. a clever or funny act 2. to cheat	**tricked** **tricking** **tricky**
trickle	to flow in a thin stream	**trickle** **trickling**
tricycle	a three-wheeled cycle	
tried	(Peter *tried* on his new boots)	
trifle	1. a sweet mixture of sponge cake, fruit or jam, custard and cream 2. something that is not worth much	
trigger	the part of a gun which you pull in order to fire the bullet	
trim	1. neat: tidy 2. to cut the rough edges off something	**trimmed** **trimming**
trip	1. an outing 2. to stumble 3. to move lightly	**tripped** **tripper** **tripping**
trod	(I slipped when I *trod* on the ice)	
trodden	(The flowers were *trodden* down by the stray horses)	
trolley	a hand-drawn cart	
trolley-bus	a 'bus that is driven by electricity from overhead wires	**trolley-buses**
trot	to run slowly	**trotted** **trotting**
trombone	a musical wind instrument	
trouble	worry: difficulty	**troublesome**
trousers	a piece of clothing with two legs to cover the body from the waist to the ankles	

trowel	1. a small spade-shaped tool used by a gardener 2. a flat-bladed tool used by a bricklayer	
truant	someone who is away from school without permission	
truck	1. a railway wagon 2. a lorry	
true	1. correct 2. real 3. faithful	**truly** **truth** **truthful** **truthfully**
trumpet	a musical wind instrument	
truncheon	a short club which a policeman sometimes carries	
trunk	1. the thick part of a tree or body 2. a large luggage box 3. the long nose of an elephant	
trust	to believe without question	**trusted** **trusting**
try	1. to give something a trial 2. to attempt	**tried** **tries** **trying**
tube	1. a long, narrow pipe 2. the underground railway in London	
tuck	1. a sewn fold in material 2. to cover snugly in bed	**tucked** **tucking**
Tuesday	the third day of the week	
tug	1. a boat used for towing 2. to pull with a jerk	**tugged** **tugging**
tulip	a plant grown from a bulb, with a flower like a small cup	
tumble	1. a sudden fall 2. to fall	**tumbled** **tumbling**
tumbler	a drinking glass	
tune	1. the music of a song 2. to make a musical instrument give the right sound	**tuned** **tuning**

tunic	1. a dress worn in school 2. the jacket part of a uniform
tunnel	a passage cut through a hill or under the ground
turban	a long piece of cloth worn wrapped around the head
turf	surface soil thickly planted with short grass
turkey	a large farmyard bird, usually eaten at Christmas
turn	1. to move round **turned** 2. to change direction or posi- **turning** tion
turnip	a plant with a round white root which is eaten as a vegetable
turnstile	a gate which turns on a centre pole and which allows one person at a time to pass through it
tusk	a very long tooth, sticking out beyond the mouth
twelve	12 **twelfth**
twenty	20 **twentieth**
twice	two times: double
twig	a very small branch
twin	one of two children in a family born at the same time
twinkle	to throw out gleams of light: to **twinkled** sparkle **twinkling**
twist	to turn round and round **twisted** **twisting**
two	2
tying	(Sally was *tying* up her shoe-lace)
typewriter	a machine with keys worked by the fingers, for writing

typhoon	a very bad storm
tyre	a rubber band put round a wheel

u

ugly	not pleasant to look at	**uglier** **ugliest** **ugliness**
ukulele	a musical instrument like a guitar	
umbrella	a round frame covered with waterproof cloth, which you use for sheltering from the rain	
umpire	someone who is in charge of a game and sees that you keep to the rules	
unable	not able to do something	
unarmed	having no weapons	
unbeaten	never defeated	
unbolt	to move back the bolt on a door or gate	**unbolted** **unbolting**
unbutton	to undo a button	**unbuttoned** **unbuttoning**
uncertain	not sure	
uncle	your mother's or your father's brother, or your aunt's husband	
uncomfortable	uneasy: not comfortable	
uncommon	unusual	
unconscious	not knowing what is going on around you	
uncork	to take the cork out of a bottle	**uncorked** **uncorking**
uncover	to take the cover off something	**uncovered** **uncovering**

undamaged   not hurt or broken in any way

undecided   when you have not made up your mind

under   below   **underneath**

underground   1. a railway that runs under the ground
2. under the ground

undergrowth   thick, low-growing bushes

underhand   secret: sly

underline   to put a line under something   **underlined underlining**

understand   to know what something means   **understand- ing understood**

undo   to untie or unfasten   **undid undoes undoing**

undress   to take clothes off   **undressed undresses undressing**

uneasy   worried: anxious: uncomfortable

unemployed   out of work

uneven   rough: not level

unfair   not just: not fair

unfasten   to undo or untie something   **unfastened unfastening**

unfit   1. not well   2. not suitable

unfold   to spread or open out   **unfolded unfolding**

unfortunate   unlucky   **unfortun- ately**

ungrateful   not thankful

unhappy   sad: miserable   **unhappily**

unhealthy   not well: in poor health

uniform   clothes worn by people who belong to a school or a special group

universe   everything that there is   **universal**

un up ur us

university	a school for higher education	universities
unkind	cruel: not kind	
unless	(You will not learn *unless* you try hard)	
unload	to take a load off something	unloaded unloading
unlock	to open a lock	unlocked unlocking
unlucky	out of luck	
unnecessary	not needed	
unnoticed	not seen	
unpack	to take the things out of a case or parcel	unpacked unpacking
unpleasant	not pleasing	
unpopular	not well liked	
unroll	to open out a roll of something	unrolled unrolling
untie	to unfasten a knot	untied untying
until	till	
unusual	not very common: rare	
unwrap	to take the cover off a parcel	unwrapped unwrapping
upon	on	
upright	standing straight up	
uproar	a great noise of shouting	
upset	to overturn or disturb	upsetting
upstairs	on the next floor up	
urgent	needing to be dealt with at once	urgently
use	1. (My friend gave me the *use* of his pen) 2. (John and Mary *use* their bicycles for the journey to school)	useful useless
usual	ordinary: common	usually

V

vacuum	a space with no air in it	
vain	too proud of yourself: conceited	
valley	a strip of low land between hills	
valuable	worth a great deal	
vanish	to disappear	**vanished** **vanishes** **vanishing**
various	different sorts	
varnish	1. a sticky liquid which gives a hard, shiny surface to things	**varnishes** **varnished**
	2. to put varnish on to something	**varnishes** **varnishing**
vase	a jar to hold flowers	
vaseline	a greasy ointment	
vast	very large	
veal	the meat from a calf	
vegetable	a plant used for food	
veil	a net covering for a woman's face	
vein	one of the tubes in the body which carry blood	
velvet	a smooth, soft, silky cloth	
verdict	judgement: decision	
verse	lines of poetry	
versus	against	
vertical	exactly upright	**vertically**
very	true: really	
vessel	1. a boat or ship	
	2. something to hold liquids	
vest	a garment worn next to the skin	
vex	to annoy	**vexed** **vexes** **vexing**

vicar   a Church of England parson in **vicarage** charge of a small district

vicious   1. spiteful
2. wicked

victory   a win   **victories**
victorious

view   what you can see

village   a small group of houses in the **villagers** country

villain   an evil person

vine   the plant on which grapes **vineyard** grow

vinegar   a sour liquid used for pickling **vinegary** and to flavour food

violet   1. a bluish-purple colour
2. a plant which has flowers of a bluish-purple colour

violin   a four-stringed musical instru- **violinist** ment played with a bow

visit   to call and see someone   **visited**
visiting
visitor

voice   you use it to talk or sing

volcano   a mountain that is made when **volcanoes** molten rock and ash are forced out through a hole in the earth's crust

volume   1. a book
2. the amount of space taken up by anything

vote   to choose someone at an elec- **voted** tion   **voter**
voting

voyage   a long journey by sea

vulture   a large bird that feeds on dead animals

W

wade	to walk through water	**waded** **wader** **wading**
wafer	a very thin biscuit	
wage	money earned by working	
wagon (**waggon**)	1. a cart used for carrying heavy loads 2. a railway truck	
waist	the middle of the body	
waistcoat	a sleeveless garment worn under a jacket	
wait for	to stay in a place until something happens	**waited** **waiting**
wait on	to serve food at a table	**waiter** **waiting** **waitress**
wake	to stop sleeping	**waking** **woke** **woken**
walk	to go on foot	**walked** **walker** **walking**
wall	1. a fence made of brick, stone or concrete 2. the side of a room or building	**walled**
wallaby	a small kangaroo	**wallabies**
wallet	a thin pocket case, usually made of leather	
walrus	a large sea animal like a seal	**walruses**
wand	a long, thin rod	
wander	to move slowly along in no special direction	**wandered** **wandering**
want	1. to need 2. to wish for	**wanted** **wanting**
war	when armies fight	

wardrobe	a tall cupboard for storing clothes	
warehouse	a building for storing things	
warm	neither hot nor cold	**warmer** **warmest** **warmly** **warmth**
warn	to tell someone about the danger of anything	**warned** **warning**
warrior	a person who has done a lot of fighting in war	
wash	to take dirt off anything by cleaning with water	**washed** **washer** **washes** **washing**
wasp	a black and yellow flying insect that stings	
waste	1. something that is useless 2. not to use up 3. to use up carelessly	**wasted** **wasteful** **wasting**
watch	1. a small clock that you wear, usually on the wrist 2. to keep your eyes fixed on something	**watches** **watched** **watches** **watching**
watchman	a person who guards a building	**watchmen**
water	a liquid which we drink	**waterless** **watery**
waterfall	a place where water tumbles from one level to another	
waterproof	not allowing water to pass through	
wave	1. a moving line of water on the sea or on a lake 2. a curve or curl in your hair 3. to flutter something	**waved** **waving** **wavy**
wax	used for making candles	
way	1. a path or road 2. how to do something	**wayside**

weak	not strong	**weaker** **weakest** **weakling** **weakly** **weakness**
wealth	all that a rich person has	**wealthier** **wealthiest** **wealthy**
weapon	a tool to fight with	
wear	1. to be dressed in something 2. to rub away	**wearing** **worn**
weary	tired	**wearily** **weariness**
weasel	a long thin wild animal	
weather	(The *weather* was sunny)	
weathercock	the shape of a cock on a pointer, which turns to show from which way the wind is blowing	
weave	to make cloth by passing threads under and over one another	**weaving** **woven**
wedding	when people get married	
Wednesday	the fourth day of the week	
weed	1. a wild plant growing where it is not wanted 2. to take out unwanted plants	**weeded** **weeding** **weed-killer**
week	seven days	**weekday** **weekend** **weekly**
weep	to cry	**weeping** **wept**
weigh	to find out how heavy anything is	**weighed** **weighing** **weight**
welcome	to show you are pleased when someone comes	**welcomed** **welcoming**

well	1. a deep hole in the ground from which water or oil can be got 2. in good health 3. in a proper manner	
wept	(The boy *wept* because his dog was lost)	
were	(John and Mary *were* six yesterday)	
west	where the sun sets: the opposite to the east	**western**
whale	a very large sea animal	
wharf	a place where ships load and unload	**wharves**
what	(Sally did not know *what* to do)	**whatever**
wheat	a plant whose seeds are used to make flour	
wheel	1. a circle of wood or metal which turns on a rod 2. to push anything on wheels	**wheeled** **wheeling**
wheelbarrow	a hand-cart with one wheel	
when	1. (I shall come in *when* it rains) 2. (*When* will you be there?)	**whenever**
where	(This is *where* I put the book)	**where-abouts** **wherever**
whether	(*Whether* we win or lose the final, we will get a medal)	
which	1. (*Which* of these is yours?) 2. (That is the desk *which* you will have)	**whichever**
while	1. (We shall be good *while* the teacher is out) 2. (In a little *while* it will be time to go)	
whip	1. a piece of thin cord or leather on a stick used for striking 2. to strike with a whip	**whipped** **whipping**

whirlwind	a very strong wind that blows round and round, and may cause great damage	
whiskers	1. hairs growing on a man's cheek 2. the long, bristly hairs which grow above the mouth on some animals	
whisper	to talk in a very quiet voice	**whispered** **whispering**
whistle	1. a wind instrument like a small pipe 2. to make a sharp high sound with the mouth	**whistled** **whistling**
white	the colour of snow	**whiter** **whitest**
whitewash	a sort of watery white paint for covering walls and ceilings	**white-washed**
who	1. (*Who* spilt the ink?) 2. (It was Jim *who* was there)	**whom** **whose**
whole	1. every part of a thing 2. undamaged: complete	
why	for what reason?	
wick	the cotton part of a candle or oil-lamp, which is lit	
wicked	evil: bad	
wicket	three stumps in a game of cricket	
wide	broad	**wider** **widest**
widow	a woman whose husband is dead	
widower	a man whose wife is dead	
width	how wide a thing is	
wife	a married woman	wives
wigwam	a tent used by Red Indians	
wild	untamed: fierce	**wildly**
wilful	1. wanting one's own way 2. done on purpose	**wilfully**

will	1. the power to choose what to do 2. (*Will* you go?)	
willing	ready to do what you are asked	**willingly**
willow	a tree which grows near water	
wilt	to droop	**wilted** **wilting**
win	to gain a victory	**winner** **winning** **won**
wind	1. air that moves quickly 2. to wrap round tightly 3. to twist in and out	**windier** **windiest** **winding** **windmill** **windscreen** **windy** **wound**
window	a space in the wall to let in air and light	**window-sill**
wine	a drink usually made from grapes or fruit	
wing	the part of a bird that is spread out when the bird flies	**winged**
wink	to move one eyelid up and down	**winked** **winking**
winter	the season between autumn and spring	**wintry**
wipe	to dry or clean something with a cloth	**wiped** **wiper** **wiping**
wire	a thin metal thread	**wired** **wireless** **wiring**
wise	sensible	**wisdom** **wisely**
wish	1. (Cinderella's *wish* was granted when she went to the Ball) 2. to want something	**wishes** **wished** **wishes** **wishful** **wishing**

witch	a woman who is supposed to do magic	**witches**
with	(Mary came to school *with* Susan)	**within** **without**
witness	someone who was watching when something happened	**witnesses**
witty	funny in a clever way	
wizard	a man who is supposed to do magic	
wobble	to rock from side to side	**wobbled** **wobbling**
woke	(The sun was shining when I *woke* up in the morning)	
wolf	a wild animal like a large dog	**wolves**
woman	a female	**women**
won	(Our team *won* the Cup)	
wonder	1. amazement 2. something causing amazement 3. to be curious	**wondered** **wonderful** **wondering**
wood	1. the trunk and branches of a tree 2. a large group of trees	**wooded** **wooden** **woodland** **woodwork**
woodpecker	a bird that taps a tree with its beak to find insects for food	
wool	1. the hairy coat of a sheep 2. the thread made from wool	**woollen** **woolly**
word	a sound or group of letters that has a definite meaning	
wore	(She *wore* a blue coat)	
work	1. a job 2. to do a job of some kind	**worked** **worker** **working** **workshop**
worker	a person who works, usually with tools	
world	the earth and everything on it	
worm	a small animal with no legs, that wriggles along	

worn	1. showing signs of wear	
	2. (I have not *worn* this hat yet)	
worry	1. care	**worries**
	2. to be troubled about some-thing	**worried** **worries**
	3. to annoy	**worrying**
worse	less good	
worst	the least good	
worth	1. of the same value as	**worthless**
	2. deserving of	**worthy**
would	(He *would* like to help me)	
wound	1. damage to the skin	**wounded**
	2. to damage someone's skin	**wounding**
	3. (John *wound* a ball of wool)	
woven	made of threads crossed over and under each other	
wrap	to cover round	**wrapped** **wrapper** **wrapping**
wreck	1. something that has been damaged or completely ruined	**wreckage** **wrecked** **wrecking**
	2. to make a wreck of some-thing	
wren	a very small bird	
wrestle	1. to try to force someone to the ground by struggling with him	**wrestled** **wrestler** **wrestling**
	2. to struggle with	
wriggle	to move by twisting and turn-ing	**wriggled** **wriggler** **wriggling**
wring	to squeeze by twisting	**wringer** **wringing** **wrung**
wrinkle	1. a crease	**wrinkled**
	2. to make a wrinkle	**wrinkling**
wrist	the joint between the hand and the arm	

write	to form words or figures so that they can be read	**writing** **written** **wrote**
wrong	not right	**wrongly**
wrote	(I *wrote* a letter to my aunt)	
wrung	(Jim *wrung* the clothes to squeeze out the water)	

X

x-rays	rays used to take photographs which show what your body is like underneath your skin
xylophone	a musical instrument made of bars of wood which are hit with hammers

y

yacht	a light boat with large sails	**yachting**
yard	1. measure of length 2. enclosed ground, usually near a building	
yawn	to take a deep breath through the mouth because you feel tired	**yawned** **yawning**
year	twelve months: fifty-two weeks: three hundred and sixty-five days: the time that the earth takes to go round the sun	**yearly**
yell	to shout or scream very loudly	**yelled** **yelling**
yellow	the colour of buttercup flowers	
yesterday	the day before today	